REGENERATIVE DEVELOPMENT AND DESIGN

A FRAMEWORK FOR EVOLVING SUSTAINABILITY

PAMELA MANG
BEN HAGGARD
REGENESIS

WILEY

Cover Design: Wiley

Cover Images: (bottom) © Flickr/Nicholas A. Tonelli, Susquehanna River; (top, left to right) © Michael Sotnikov, Cheonggyecheong Festival; Courtesy of Playa Viva © David Leventhal; Teachers © Regenesis Group; © Sasaki Associates, Las Salinas Master Plan

This book is printed on acid-free paper.

Published by John Wiley & Sons, Inc., Hoboken, New Jersey
Published simultaneously in Canada

For general information about our other products and services, please contact our Customer Care Department within the United States at (800) 762-2974, outside the United States at (317) 572-3993 or fax (317) 572-4002.

Wiley publishes in a variety of print and electronic formats and by print-on-demand. Some material included with standard print versions of this book may not be included in e-books or in print-on-demand. If this book refers to media such as a CD or DVD that is not included in the version you purchased, you may download this material at http://booksupport.wiley.com. For more information about Wiley products, visit www.wiley.com.

Library of Congress Cataloging-in-Publication Data:

9781118972861 (pbk); 978-1-118-97291-5 (ebk);
978-1-118-97292-2 (ebk); 978-1-119-14969-9 (ebk)

Printed in the United States of America

SKY10026920_050721

CONTENTS

Premise: *Every living system has inherent within it the possibility to move to new levels of order, differentiation, and organization.*

Principle: *Design for evolution.*

Premise: *Co-evolution among humans and natural systems can only be undertaken in specific places, using approaches that are precisely fitted to them.*

Principle: *Partner with place.*

Premise: *The sustainability of a living system is tied directly to its beneficial integration into a larger system.*

Principle: *Call forth a collective vocation.*

Premise: *Projects should be vehicles for catalyzing the cooperative enterprises required to enable evolution.*

Principle: *Actualize stakeholder systems toward co-evolving mutualism.*

Premise: *Potential comes from evolving the value-generating capacity of a system to make unique contributions to the evolution of larger systems.*

Principle: *Work from potential, not problems.*

Premise: *The continuing health of living systems depends on each member living out its distinctive role.*

Principle: *Find your distinctive, value-adding roles.*

Premise: *Small conscious and conscientious interventions in the right place can create beneficial, system-wide effects.*

Principle: *Leverage systemic regeneration by making nodal interventions.*

Premise: *A project can only create systemic benefit within a field of caring, co-creativity, and co-responsibility.*

Principle: *Design the design process to be developmental.*

Premise: *The actualization of a self requires the simultaneous development of the systems of which it is a part.*

Principle: *Become a systems actualizer.*

FOREWORD

Predictions of the future can be hazardous or downright foolish. But the failure of foresight—the inability to read the hand-writing on the wall—is even more so. Designers of all kinds work in the conflicted space between these two poles. Their goal is to improve small parts of a rapidly changing world with the tools of form, scale, materials, energy, water, color, landscape, and the creativity that is found most often at the grassroots level. But what needs to be improved?

The short answer is "a great deal," including an energy system that is rapidly destabilizing the climate, an economy driving tens of thousands of species to extinction, a political system that sanctions gross inequality, an uncivil society, the growing autism toward the natural world, and a global system mired in conflict. These are related problems, parts of a larger civilizational crisis with roots traceable to the seventeenth century authors of the mechanical world view. But there are deeper pathologies with footprints back to our ancient schizophrenia toward the natural world that had to be tamed a bit before it could be appreciated.

Designers, however, typically do not work at the macro scale of civilization for good reasons. Whether as architecture, engineering, materials, or landscapes, design is bounded by the minute particulars of projects in their specific social, cultural, and historical context. As a result designers work from the bottom up on projects at the building, neighborhood, and city scales. But the big problems mentioned above are in large part the sum total of bad design (including that of public policies) at lower levels. There are many reasons for bad design, not the least of which is a professional focus on form-making, often oblivious to other consequences.

Beginning in the 1970s a few renegade architects like Sim Van der Ryn in California became concerned about the collateral environmental impacts of the design professions. Van der Ryn envisioned ecological design as the calibration of buildings with their places, which required further integral understanding of landscapes, energy flows, waste cycling, materials, sunlight, water, and ecological processes. Ecological design, in other words, aims to calibrate human actions with the way natural systems work as particular places, larger landscapes, and whole ecologies. It aims to work with, not against, the flows of energy and natural cycling of materials. The goal, in short, was to reduce environmental impacts of the "built environment" in a civilization that prized economic expansion above all else with hardly a thought for the morrow.

What began so modestly in the 1970s has rapidly grown into a global movement to harmonize buildings, neighborhoods, and cities with the surrounding nature. After the publication of the Brundtland Commission report in 1987, the goals of ecological designers expanded to embrace the wider (but vague) mission of sustainability. But we know now that that word signifies more than was once assumed. Sustainability is the sum total of other qualities. As Chattanooga City Councilman, David Crockett puts it: "make it clean, green, safe, and fair and it will be sustainable." The left side of that equation, however, requires the elimination of the growing inequality that is a precursor to violence and ruined lives. It further requires rethinking our core assumptions about the relation between economic growth and real progress. Ecological design, in other words, must be large enough in foresight, scope, and heart to include the social and economic environment in which it is embedded. In that way ecological design is a radical endeavor in the true sense of the word, it gets to the root of what ails us.

The work described in this book takes design to yet another level that aims to regenerate the fabric of life and repair the wounds and tears inflicted by the carelessness of the fossil-fuel-powered growth economy. Regenerative design strives to create the conditions of health which ecologist Aldo Leopold once defined as "the capacity of the land for self-renewal." It aims, in other words, for wholeness, a word linked etymologically with healing, health, and Holy. Designers in this sense are midwives to the birth of a larger, deeper, and more resilient kind of order capable of regenerating the conditions of life and health. It is predicated on the co-evolution of human and natural systems, each supporting the other. In Robert Grudin's words, design, "unlike any other concept . . . calls for us to create a unity of part with whole, a concord of form and function, a finished product that is harmonious with society and with nature."[1]

In this history the trend is for design questions to go to deeper levels and design projects to become catalysts for still further changes. In architect Stuart Walker's words design must, "transcend utility and conventional function-led, and especially technology-led approaches."[2] Designers, in his view, must rise above "the calculated creation of dissatisfaction" and "think more comprehensively about the products we already produce and their implications."[3] Design, in other words, must be an act of integration, not just specialization, with the goal of creating a wholeness that includes spiritual well-being. And it should start with those who serve as designers.[4]

Regenerative design has many effects. For one, it changes the relationship of people to their places. It can restore the reservoir of practical ecological competence at the local level allowing us to do more for ourselves and for each other—the things that we once did naturally as capable people, good neighbors, and active citizens. It helps ground us by better informing us of where we are and the ecology and energy flows by which we are sustained in a particular place. In a world where any one place has come to look much like any other, we have lost sight of the fine print of our lives and how we are provisioned with food, energy, materials, and spiritual sustenance.

We are mostly ignorant of the costs and consequences of the systems that provide for us so seamlessly and oblivious to their inherent fragility. Regenerative design helps us know where we are and how to be competent, respectful, and generous there. Our places should be ecologically designed landscapes whose multiple functions retain water for drought periods, manage floods, grow food and fiber, sustain wildlife, and absorb carbon. They should be working systems that blend agro-forestry, mixed-use permacultures, intensive agricultural and gardening zones, viticulture, aquaculture, water purification, restoration, and recreation. And they should be loved and managed by local citizens who use them to train young people in the essentials of managed integrated ecologies.[5]

Further, regenerative design should enhance the opportunities for caring, conviviality, celebration, and face-to-face democracy.[6] Communities with front porches, public squares, community gardens and solar systems, neighborhood stores, corner pubs, and open places of worship are more likely to thrive in the years ahead. This is because they create the conditions favorable to neighborliness, community cohesion, and buffering from hardships. Good design should engage people in the making of their homes, neighborhoods, towns, and regions. It should increase civic intelligence, sense of potential, and joy in life. In this way, designers are facilitators in a larger public conversation, architects of better possibilities, not just makers of buildings and things.

A rapidly warming climate will add to the design challenges ahead. Designers must reckon with a world of higher temperatures, stronger winds, more frequent and larger storms, rising ocean levels, longer droughts, much larger rainfall events, and new diseases.[7] These will likely cause interruptions in supplies of food, energy, and water and could trigger social disruptions. We must design with the awareness of the fragility of our civilization, as Jared Diamond and others warn. We must build in the ability to maintain hope and function as a society in emergency (and possibly breakdown) and lay the basis for recovery.[8]

The Great Work of our generation is to create a post-fossil-fuel and post-consumer economy that is regenerative, fair, durable, resilient, convivial, and democratic. It must be powered by renewable energy. It must be a circular economy that recycles, reuses, or transforms its wastes. Of necessity it will be much more focused on essentials of food, energy, shelter, clean water, education, the arts, and rootedness in place and bioregion. It will be built by local people who cherish and understand their places and the place of nature in a sustainable economy. But it must also be a political economy, a product of revitalized grassroots capability and vision. If it is to flourish, it must regenerate possibilities and capacities that grow from foresight married to practical ecological competence.

David W. Orr

ENDNOTES

1. Robert Grudin, *Design and Truth* (New Haven: Yale University Press, 2010) p. 131.
2. Stuart Walker, *Designing Sustainability* (London: Routledge, 2014) p. 35; also Victor Papenek, *Design for the Real World*, 2nd ed. (Chicago: Academy Chicago Publishers, 1984/1992) p. 252.
3. *Ibid.*, pp. 47, 45.
4. Papenek, op. cit., pp. 293–299.
5. Modeled on John and Nancy Todd's work in ecological design, the Intervale project in Burlington, Vermont is a prime example.
6. Randolph T. Hester, *Design for Ecological Democracy* (Cambridge: MIT Press, 2006), is a thorough guide to "ecological democracy" and the use of design to rebuild the sinews of a coherent, participatory, and therefore resilient society.
7. Sue Roaf et.al., *Adapting Buildings and Cities for Climate Change*, 2nd edition (London: Elsevier, 2009); Alisdair McGregor et.al., *Two Degrees: The Built Environment and Our Changing Climate* (London: Routledge, 2013).
8. For example, Lewis Dartnell, *The Knowledge: How to Rebuild Civilization in the Aftermath of a Cataclysm* (New York: Penguin Books, 2014).

ACKNOWLEDGMENTS

We'd like to give thanks to our colleagues at Regenesis who "authored" the work introduced here through *their* work over the past 20 years—Joel Glanzberg, Bob Mang, Nicholas Mang, Tim Murphy, Bill Reed, and our newest member Ray Lucchesi.

We'd also like to acknowledge our writing team, without whom this book would never have seen the light of day: Shannon Murphy, our multitalented business manager whose editing sharpened our writing and whose project management kept the whole show on the road; Kit Brewer, copyeditor supreme, who made our sentences elegant and brought order and harmony to the text; and Adriane Zacmanidis, who brought her expressive gifts to the task of developing, selecting, and assembling the images and illustrations for the book.

We have the utmost gratitude for our respective spouses, Bob Mang and Joe Miron, whose remarkable patience and ongoing support kept us going.

And, finally, we thank the many people whose work has inspired us to dig deeper and go further over the years, and on whose shoulders we stand. Our work has been particularly sourced by the thinking of Charlie Krone. In some ways he triggered this journey with his statement 30 years ago that regeneration must be the work of the twenty-first century.

Other thinkers who have influenced us include Gregory Bateson, John Bennett, Wendell Berry, David Bohm, Fritjof Capra, Ervin Laszlo, John Tillman Lyle, Bill Mollison, David Orr, Robert Rodale, Elisabet Sahtouris, Carol Sanford, and E.O. Wilson. In addition, we have been nourished and inspired by the spirit of exploration and committed engagement that we find in friends and colleagues such as Bob Berkebile, John Boecker, Chrisna DuPlessis, Dominique Hes, Jason McLennan, Sym Van der Ryn, Judy Wick, and our students and clients around the planet who are striving to bring a more regenerative world into being.

The work of these visionaries continues to inspire and support us as we move on to the next horizon in our own learning and growth.

CHANGING OUR MINDS

Throughout history, the really fundamental changes in societies have come not from dictates of governments and the results of battles but through vast numbers of people changing their minds—sometimes by only a little bit. . . . By deliberately changing the internal images of reality, people can change the world.[1]

Willis Harmon

In the twenty-first century, human beings face global and seemingly intractable problems. However, close examination reveals that the challenges lie not in the problems themselves, but in the inherent complexity of the world within which they exist.

Most of the technologies needed to address these problems have been developed and are well understood, and yet they persist because their causes are systemic and can't be solved at a purely technical level. They require a different kind of mind, one that can creatively navigate multiple overlapping systems—economic, social, ecological, and political.

One could argue, for example, that the solution to the problem of deforestation is simple: "Plant trees." As a technology, tree planting generates beneficial results with regard to everything from climate change to degraded ecosystems to people's quality of life. Yet it has proven very difficult to summon the political will and financial resources necessary to make a commitment to reversing environmental decline through broad-scale tree planting. The technology might be simple, but managing the complex interactions among political, economic, and ecological dynamics in order to put the technology to use? That's another matter.

> The important global challenges of our time will be solved through widespread adoption of design practices that are capable of assessing and responding to the world's living complexity.

The challenges of our time will be solved through widespread adoption of design practices that are capable of assessing and responding to the world's living complexity. Regenerative development provides a framework for growing this capability.

REGENERATIVE DEVELOPMENT

The Regenesis Group first proposed the term *regenerative development* in 1995. It describes an approach that is about enhancing the ability of living beings to co-evolve, so that our planet continues to express its potential for diversity, complexity, and creativity.

> The core issue, Regenesis proposed, was cultural and psychological, and only secondarily technological.

The founders of Regenesis began with a fundamental belief that environmental problems were symptoms of a fractured relationship between people and nature. The core issue, they proposed, was cultural and psychological, rather than technological. Addressing it would require a transformation in how humans played their role as members of an ecologically connected planet. We would need to shift from seeing ourselves as separate from nature to seeing ourselves as part of a co-evolutionary whole, in symbiotic relationship with the living places we inhabit.

They further proposed that this shift is directly connected to will and agency. Managing the level of complexity that we are faced with requires consistent effort. For this reason, questions of individual and political will lie at the heart of many of the challenges we face as a species. If we don't address intangibles like motivation and will, the tangible solutions that seem so obvious will continue to elude us.

The theoretical and technological foundations for a regenerative development methodology emerged as Regenesis engaged its clients and colleagues in the practical challenges of land and community development. The goal was a meta-discipline for integrating a broad range of ecological and social dynamics.

This work drew from the backgrounds of Regenesis' members, which included architecture, business, landscape ecology, geohydrology, landscape design, regenerative agriculture, real estate development, urban planning, general systems theory, living systems theory, and developmental psychology. It integrated three distinct but complementary approaches to change:

- Living Systems Thinking: a framework-based approach, developed by Charles Krone, that consciously improves people's capacity to illuminate the inherent potential that a living system is attempting to manifest
- Permaculture: an ecological design system, originated by Bill Mollison and David Holmgren in the 1970s, that discerns patterns in natural and human systems in order to weave them together as dynamic wholes
- Developmental Change Processes: an approach to community engagement that encourages stakeholders to work together to evolve the potential of place, rather than struggling over the limits presented by existing conditions

WE ARE ALL DESIGNERS

Those who are drawn to the practice of regenerative development tend to share certain characteristics. They feel a deep connection to natural systems. They recognize that a sustainable future requires transforming not just physical infrastructure but social structures as well. They believe that how decisions are made is fundamental to creating real change, and they seek to work developmentally and co-creatively with those they serve. They make thoughtful choices about which actions are likely to be the most systemically beneficial. Put another way, they are designers.

Although this book is addressed primarily to designers working on human habitation, the principles articulated here are applicable to the design of almost anything—from industrial products to forest management plans,

educational curricula to transportation infrastructures, community economies to businesses. In other words, because design is a nearly universal
human activity, this book is not just for architects, planners, engineers, or
community organizers. Its principles can be applied by all those who wish
to better the health and well-being of their communities. Educators and
businesspeople, investors and community leaders, farmers and foresters,
architects and engineers—all have necessary contributions to make to a
regenerative way of living.

> . . . because design is a nearly universal human activity . . . its prin-
> ciples can be applied by all those who wish to better the health and
> well-being of their communities.

The purpose of this book is to provide a user-friendly introduction to the nature
of thinking that is fundamental to regenerative development. Through real-
world examples and general principles, it provides a framework for rethinking what design and development have the potential to accomplish. From a
regenerative perspective, any project, no matter how modest, can generate
beneficial impacts that ripple out and contribute to making a healthier world.

Because this practice was first evolved in arenas of land use and community
development, the vast majority of the examples offered in the following
chapters are drawn from these fields. However, regenerative development
is organized around a set of design principles that are broadly applicable.
Design, after all, is the application of forethought to something we wish to
achieve. Teachers design curricula, activists design community engagements,
and doctors design medical protocols in much the same ways that planners
design town centers.

Regenerative development lies outside of the mechanistic habits of thought
that are cultivated and sustained by most educational, social, and economic
institutions. This means that regenerative development can feel elusive and
challenging at first. Its language can seem opaque, its meanings slippery and
hard to grasp, because words are being used in unfamiliar ways, marked by
the continuous flow and change that is characteristic of living, evolving systems. But even so, regenerative development can be understood by anyone

with the will to engage with it. Our human minds, with their elegance and power, are the products of the same evolutionary flow and change as every other living system. Nature, one might say, is our nature.

AN INVITATION

The thinking behind regenerative development continues to evolve through project work and in dialogue with diverse sustainability practitioners. A core aim of this book is to extend an invitation to join in that exploration. Regenerative development is itself a co-evolutionary process that will continue to deepen and ramify as new practitioners, disciplines, and cultures bring their perspectives to defining a new, participatory role for human beings on a rapidly changing planet. We at Regenesis see ourselves as part of a tradition that started before us and will continue long after us. The journey is only beginning.

> The present moment offers the potential, born of crisis, to transform the way humans inhabit Earth.

The present moment offers the potential, born of crisis, to transform the way humans inhabit Earth. To do so, we must learn to respond creatively to an increasingly unpredictable world. We must enable the places where we live and work to thrive, not just sustain a precarious balance. We must embrace the inherently beautiful complexity of life as a source of innovation and evolution. We must discover new ways to participate in a dynamic universe.

An old Sufi story beautifully captures our historic moment: *There once was a man who was renowned in his village and the surrounding region for his wisdom. Two young jackanapes decided to test him. "Let's catch a small bird," said one to the other. "We'll ask him if it's alive or dead. If he says it's alive, I'll crush it in my hands. If he says it's dead, I'll let it fly away and prove him wrong." When they approached the sage, the youth called out, "Old man, hidden in my hands is a bird. You have great wisdom. Can you tell me if it is dead or alive?" The wise man looked him in the eyes, and with a gentle smile replied, "It is in your hands."*

Our destiny? It is in our hands.

FIGURE A.1 Our destiny? It is in our hands.
Copyright © Nathan Siemers/flickr.com Creative Commons

ENDNOTE

1. Willis Harmon, *Global Mind Change: The Promise of the Last Years of the Twentieth Century* (New York: Warner Books, 1990), pp. 155, 157.

THE FUTURE OF SUSTAINABILITY

*We have an incredible opportunity to improve life
on this planet for all living beings.*[1]

Daniel Wildcat

Over the last decade and a half, the global sustainability movement has grown more rapidly every year. Aided by blockbuster films, startup industries, and widening impacts of climate change, the practice of sustainability has shifted from twentieth-century geeky backwater to twenty-first-century international dialogue. Cities around the world are in a race to show who can be greenest quickest. Businesses tout their sustainable practices as a marketing advantage. Green products compete for shelf space in retail markets with a war of adjectives—natural, holistic, organic, sustainably harvested, fair trade. Today the debate is shifting from *whether* we should work on sustainability to *how* we're going to get it done.

This focused attention has led to an explosion of creative activity and new methodologies: cradle-to-cradle, natural step, permaculture, biophilia, living buildings, eco-districts, resilience planning, transition cities, and integrative and biomimetic design. But a superabundance of options for what we *can* do has also made figuring out what we *should* do more challenging (Figure B.1).

Professionals and citizen activists alike find themselves challenged: "How do all these approaches fit together?" "How do they connect with my work?" "How should I choose among them?" "How can I know that they are leading to a more sustainable world?"

To successfully access and employ the power of this rapidly changing field, we must see the relationships among these varied strategies and how they fit together. This becomes possible through an integrative framework called *regenerative development*.

FIGURE B.1 A growing cornucopia of green design choices makes it ever more challenging for designers to sort what we *should* do from what we *can* do.

Copyright © Regenesis Group Inc. Illustration by Kronosphere Design

To successfully access and employ the power of this rapidly changing field, we must see the relationships among varied strategies and how to fit them together.

Regenerative development provides a context and guide for understanding the multiplicity of sustainability approaches as a coherent phenomenon that is genuinely capable of matching the complexity of today's global issues.

A GROWING NEED FOR INTEGRATION

Analysts typically trace such rapid growth in a modern industry to the rise of global communications or the economic incentives of new markets. But in this case there is a deeper explanation. The primary driving force behind the growth of sustainability has come *from Earth itself.* Whatever one believes about the causes, it is evident that every one of our critical planetary support systems—oceans, forests, soils, atmosphere, biodiversity—is in decline. It is even more evident that all of our best efforts have failed to halt the degenerative spirals that are sapping the health of these systems and, in the process, threatening the viability of human communities.

Since the turn of the century, cascades of scientific studies have been painting an increasingly grim picture of the state of the planet. Loss of biological diversity has reduced the ability of ecosystems to sustain human societies.[2] Sixty percent of ecosystem services such as water supplies, fish stocks, fertile soils, and storm protection are already in decline.[3] Between 1970 and 2010 vertebrate populations around the world (mammals, birds, reptiles, amphibians, and fish) dropped by more than half in fewer than two human generations.[4]

In Latin America the decline is even more drastic—83 percent. Fifty countries are experiencing "moderate to severe water stress on a year-round basis." Twenty-seven countries—including the United Kingdom, Switzerland, Austria, Norway, and the Netherlands—are importing more than half the water they consume in order to produce goods from wheat to cotton. Fourteen of the top 20 U.S. cities (40 percent of the world's population, nearly 1.2 billion people) are located in coastal zones where a changing climate exposes them to the risk of storm surges and sea level rises.[5]

Sustainability is no longer an issue of altruism or responsibility; it has become one of survival. "Nature," notes pioneer ecologist Lawrence Slobodkin, "doesn't die. But the planet may no longer be a welcome place for human habitation."[6]

WHAT IS SUSTAINABILITY—REALLY?

The sustainability movement continues to be handicapped, decades after its emergence, by a lingering lack of clarity about what *sustainability* actually means. When pressed, most people agree that sustainable human endeavors are those that can be maintained over a long period of time without causing problems for future generations. They also generally agree that sustainability is going to require fundamental changes in the ways humans live. But then the conversation goes straight to strategizing. What's usually missing is an adequate understanding of what sustainability is actually supposed to achieve.

The Urban Learning Group has observed that, "When tools and strategies are the initial focus of efforts to seed fundamental change, people tend to end up in the same place as they started, with little or no fundamental change."[7] In our action-oriented modern culture, we jump to devise a solution as soon as we see a problem. We try to discover the way to sustainability through a process of elimination—pick a strategy, pursue it until its usefulness has been exhausted, then switch to another. Or worse, we stand around and argue about which strategy to choose in the first place. Because we don't know where we're going, any path will do.

We can continue like this, but the risk of arriving too late increases every day.

TWO MODELS OF NATURE

A lack of clarity is hardly surprising, given that the rubric of sustainability has expanded over time to include everything from eliminating pollution to raising nations out of poverty. Practitioners might work on mitigating damage from the past or on generating radical new insights into how biological processes can inform design.

To define sustainability—*what* we are trying to sustain, and the *ability* that is therefore required—we need to begin by looking at our assumptions about how the world works. In his seminal work, *Regenerative Design for Sustainable Development*, John Tillman Lyle wrote, "All design of the human environment is based on some fundamental model of the essential character of nature deeply imbedded in the culture—the nature of nature."[8] Underlying most sustainability debates in the past 50 years are two distinct models of nature.

The first of these models coalesced in the seventeenth and eighteenth centuries around the ideas of Francis Bacon, Sir Isaac Newton, and Renee Descartes. In it, nature is finite, linear, and subject to the same laws as mechanical systems. Humans stand apart from and hold stewardship over nature for the purpose of maintaining and growing human welfare. Although this mechanistic image has been largely discredited by the changing science of the twentieth and twenty-first centuries, it continues to dominate efforts to define sustainability and articulate its tools, strategies, and goals.

The second model is drawn from the insights of ecology. In it nature works as a dynamic organic web, within which interdependent entities organize and maintain themselves, exchange information and energy, and evolve in harmony with their local environments. This model is biocentric, based on the principle that all life forms have intrinsic value and the right to exist. Humans are simply one species among many, equal rather than superior.

The philosophy of reciprocity, interdependence, and the sacredness of life is threaded throughout human history. It can be found in indigenous cultures, permeates the works of eighteenth- and nineteenth-century romantic naturalists, and informs a growing number of contemporary philosophers and scholars.

From the perspective of mechanistic thinking, our current environmental crisis is the result of mismanagement and failure to understand and observe planetary limits while pursuing human ends. It can be managed by eco-efficiency and clean technologies, increasingly accurate scientific analyses and predictions, and more enlightened oversight mandated by new, globally enforced standards, policies, and regulations.

In contrast, ecological thinking posits that the challenges to sustainability are as much psychological and spiritual as they are technical and environmental. Humans brought about the current crisis when we forgot that we belonged to and depended upon the infinitely complex web of life. In the words of David Suzuki, we stopped "seeing ourselves as physically and spiritually connected to family, clan and land."[9] From this perspective, sustainability depends on rediscovering our role as a part of nature. Thus, it requires a profound shift in our values and behaviors and new ways of seeing ourselves.

These two models appear to contradict one another. However, one can view them instead as developmental stages toward a conscious integration of humans into the community of all living beings. With this insight, the tools of the mechanistic model can be reconceived as instruments for creating a truly sustainable future.

THE CHANGING MEANING OF SUSTAINABILITY

The *New Oxford American Dictionary* defines evolution as "the gradual development of something, especially from a simple to a more complex form." Our understanding of sustainability is evolving as practitioners search for ways to engage with the full complexity of a living world. One can discern three overlapping phases in this evolution, each folding into and providing a platform for the subsequent phase, and each shaped by a different scope, frame of reference, and implied definition of sustainability.

Equilibrium

Initially, sustainability was viewed as a *steady state of equilibrium*. From this perspective, there is a threshold limit below which we can stay by achieving the right balance of inputs and outputs. If humans can maintain this state then we can go on forever, generation after generation. Most sustainability approaches of the last couple of decades are grounded in this vision, which attempts to figure out the right mix of activities to keep things running smoothly. This way of thinking about sustainability is reflected in the well-known definition contained in the 1987 Brundtland Report, commissioned by the United Nations to rally countries to work on sustainable development together: "Sustainable development is development that meets the needs of the present without compromising the ability of future generations to meet their own needs."

Design strategies for achieving sustainable equilibrium began by focusing on efficiency and the minimization of the negative impacts of resource and energy use. As the power and reach of green technologies has grown, the goal has been extended to net-neutral or net-zero—buildings, cities, and industries that have no negative effect on their environment. Because bringing human activities into balance with natural systems doesn't correct past damage, a new goal has been articulated in recent years: net-positive, where the result of our activities yields a surplus, for example, of clean energy or renewed resources.

Over the last two decades, the green design movement has become an effective instrument for creating physical structures and products that do less and less harm to living systems. There is no question that this is a critically important step toward halting the degeneration of the biosphere. At the same time, living systems science is providing mounting evidence that the goal of steady-state equilibrium in a living world is technically and philosophically untenable. Living systems simply don't exist in steady states. They survive by changing and adapting, seeking *dynamic equilibrium* within their evolving environments.

> Biologically, life is not maintenance or restoration of equilibrium but is essentially maintenance of disequilibria . . . Reaching equilibrium means death and consequent decay . . . [A] living organism becomes a body in decay when tensions and forces keeping it from equilibrium have stopped.[11]

Living systems *require* disruption to remain healthy—for example, many forests need to be renewed periodically by fire. Basing our sustainability strategies on achieving equilibrium, no matter how powerful and sophisticated our technologies become, fails to take into account the critical role of disequilibrium in living processes.

Resilience

This realization has paved the way for a second phase, in which sustainability is viewed as *resilience*. Design for resilience seeks to maintain the health and productivity of systems in the face of unpredictable changes arising in the environment. The resilience approach acknowledges that change is nonlinear, that it emerges from complex relationships among multiple actors. Living entities sustain themselves through constant adaptation to their environments. Humans and ecosystems are interdependent, and the resilience of human communities requires the resilience of the natural communities that we depend upon.

This compelling idea is growing in popularity and influence. For most of the twentieth century, resilience was the province of conservation-minded ecologists, concerned about preservation and restoration of natural systems. In the early twenty-first century, the increasing occurrence of costly, high visibility natural disasters has brought the need for resilience into sharp focus. In the process it is providing a new definition of sustainability, based not on achieving a steady state but rather on being able to regroup and move forward when equilibrium has been disrupted.

However, the resilience approach arises from the metaphor of a world spinning out of control and can result in a complex game of avoidance and rapid recovery. In such a world, politics and economics are defensive. Think of the sophisticated engineering currently under consideration to help coastal cities survive and work around the new realities of storm surge. Proposals to protect New York from future weather disasters include an eight-mile, 10-foot-high stretch of concrete, grass-topped protective barriers around the southern half of Manhattan, a "necklace" of breakwaters around Staten Island, and a $5.9 billion floodgate spanning the shallow gap of water between Long Island and New Jersey.[12]

Ironically, this bunker mentality can actually contribute to the instability it is intended to address, as the integrity of larger systems gets sacrificed to immediate local needs. After Hurricane Katrina, New Orleans looks to a 130-mile system of levees, walls, and gates to keep out a 100-year storm surge. Yet, as geology professor Anne Jefferson notes, "The extensive leveeing of the Lower Mississippi River made the 1927 floods worse, just as all levees today carry consequences for current and future floods. While levees are good for individual communities in small- to moderate-sized events, levees are bad for the river system's overall capacity to deal with flood flows."[13]

Co-evolution

In its third phase, sustainability is coming to be understood as *co-evolution*, wherein humans contribute to the abundance of life. Human communities have often been able to prosper when they worked in partnership with nature. We are gradually rediscovering this fundamental truth and imagining ways to apply it in the post-industrial age. From the perspective of co-evolution, instead of being outsiders, we humans have our own distinctive value-adding role to play within nature. This image of the role of humans has recently begun to move from the margins of the sustainability conversation to its center.

Prior to contact with industrial culture, many indigenous communities interacted with their environments in ways that increased biodiversity and productivity. John Muir believed that much of California was a pristine, untouched wilderness before the arrival of Europeans. Kat Anderson, the national ethnoecologist of the U. S. Department of Agriculture's Natural Resources Conservation Service, reveals a very different story in her book *Tending the Wild: Native American Knowledge and the Management of California's Natural Resources*.[14] Beautiful vistas that Muir mistook for wilderness were actually fertile gardens created and carefully tended over centuries by the Sierra Miwok and Valley Yokuts Indians. Reweaving natural and human communities allows us to pursue this same kind of abundance, while incorporating twenty-first-century advances and insights.

Partnering for co-evolution requires a whole-systems reorientation that connects human activities with the evolution of natural systems. In the words of Raymond Cole, an eminent theorist at the University of British Columbia, this means moving from designing things to designing "the 'capability' of the constructed world (and of human activities) to support the positive co-evolution of human and natural systems."[15] For example, oyster reefs are excellent storm surge protectors, water filters, habitat providers, and food producers. But renewing these vital and hardworking living systems will require many changes, from how we maintain and navigate our ports to the kinds of chemicals we flush into waterways to new technologies for seeding and harvesting the reefs themselves. Although these changes will pose challenges, they will also become opportunities for new forms of economic and cultural activity.

REGENERATIVE DEVELOPMENT

The concept, "co-evolutionary partner with nature," can at first seem overwhelming and hard to get one's mind around. Regenerative development provides a coherent approach for establishing this partnership by pursuing sustainability within the conceptual framework of living, evolving systems. It works on developing the capability of living systems, social as well as natural, to express their potential for diversity, complexity, and creativity.

In their 2009 study for New Zealand's Ministry for the Environment, Sarah Jenkin and Maibritt Pedersen Zari write that regenerative development "investigates how humans can participate in ecosystems through development, to create optimum health for both human communities (physically, psychologically, socially, culturally and economically) and other living organisms and systems."[16] They describe regenerative development as defining the desired outcome and regenerative design as the means of achieving it.

Understanding regenerative development in practice, rather than only in theory, requires the introduction of three key ideas: *regeneration as enabler of evolution, working in place,* and *developmental processes.*

REGENERATION AS ENABLER OF EVOLUTION

Understood as an aspect of living systems, regeneration is one of four different natures of work. All four are necessary in order for an entity to sustain itself in a world that is nested, dynamic, complex, interdependent, and evolving. Pioneering organizational consultant Charles Krone developed a framework that defines these different levels of work within a hierarchy (Figure B.2). Work at the lower levels is focused on existence (what is already manifested); at the higher levels it is concerned with potential (what could be but is not yet manifested). In this schema, the highest or regenerative level of work guides the other levels, enabling the system as a whole to evolve in harmony with its environment.

The levels of work framework allow practitioners to design for the integrated evolution of all work. It also provides a lens for seeing how and where different sustainability strategies fit and how they can be leveraged when aligned around a regenerative goal.

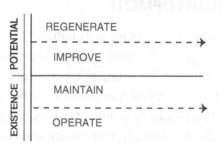

FIGURE B.2 Levels of work. Every living system engages in work that is essential to its continuing capacity for evolution. *Operating* and *maintaining* are focused on current existence; they increase performance and efficiency. *Improving* and *regenerating* introduce potential life and creativity, advancing the whole.

Copyright © Regenesis Group, Inc. Illustration by Kronosphere Design

To *operate* is to increase the efficiency of energy and material use, remove variances such as toxicity, and achieve higher standards through capable and disciplined practice. This level of work has been the green building movement's primary focus for much of its history, and many of its greatest accomplishments (such as nontoxic materials, buildings that consume no energy, and cradle-to-cradle manufacturing) have been the result.

To *maintain* means to be concerned with sustaining the desired effect and effectiveness of operations in the face of perturbations and environmental uncertainty. Efforts concerned with resilience work are at this level. One example is the Transition Movement's focus on longevity as it seeks to help communities adjust to new climate realities while shifting away from fossil fuel dependence. Educational efforts aimed at helping the public choose appropriate behaviors in relationship to wild species or ecosystems are also focused on this level of work—for example, many fire departments offer programs to educate people who live at the interface between urban and wild landscapes about fire ecology.

At the *improve* level, the focus shifts to increasing the value-adding capacity of human and natural systems. Permaculture, Holistic Management, and other ecological design systems that emphasize the development of self-organizing, highly productive agricultural ecosystems offer good examples.

For most of its history, the Quivira Coalition has worked at the improve level. A New Mexico-based nonprofit, Quivira holds a vision of harmony among humans and natural systems. It was founded at the time of the grazing "wars" of the 1990s, when ranchers and environmentalists were locked in an escalating conflict over the future of the west's public lands. Quivira brought together ranchers, conservationists, public land stewards, and scientists in a neutral place to work on this critical issue. Together they discovered a "radical center," where values aligned and differences could be reconciled.

Over time, this coalition has pushed for the adoption of new and progressive land management practices, helping to energize a national resurgence of agrarianism committed to regenerating working landscapes and rural communities. In the process, millions of acres of wildlife habitat on western rangelands have been improved and the viability of ranching and family farming as valued ways to make a living has been partially restored. A growing Quivira community has come to understand that land and people are inseparable—"economics based on nature's model of herbivory are inescapably intertwined with healthy ecosystems."[17]

At the fourth level, work that *regenerates* addresses the unrealized potential inherent in the relationship between a given system and the larger systems within which it is nested. That is, it enables living systems to evolve by expressing their latent potential in the form of new value in the world. In this way, what exists now can move toward what could be in the future. Regeneration produces a field within which the improvement of living systems can take place and provides a coalescing direction for the other levels of work. Quivira's effectiveness at improve level work owes much to the initial regenerate level work that enabled both environmentalists and ranchers to see new potential in the relationship between ranching and healthy landscapes.

The Quesada Gardens Initiative was launched in San Francisco in 2002, when one person took the simple step of planting flowers along a driveway. At the time, Quesada Avenue was ground zero for drug dealers and gang warfare in Bayview-Hunters Point on the southern industrial edge of the city. The neighborhood had long been plagued by poverty, pollution, and violent crime. In a place that hope seemed to have abandoned, one person's quiet act inspired a regenerative neighborhood initiative.

In a short time, another neighbor began planting vegetables and flowers along the block. Soon others joined in, and a trash-filled median was transformed into a community garden. Thirteen years later, this place-sourced effort has involved thousands of residents and created teaching and learning gardens, food-producing backyards, public art, gathering places, and family events. The Quesada Gardens Initiative starts "with people, and with their unique experience of the place where they live." As a result, each effort is a singular project "built from the unique needs and strengths of people where they live."[18] Collectively, they are retelling the story of Bayview-Hunters Point by tapping community wisdom and potential that before had gone unrecognized.

The four levels of work are interdependent and necessary to one another. Failure to skillfully manage work at the two lower levels can easily threaten a project or organization's very existence, usually by depleting the larger systems in which it resides. Many a project that was intended to stimulate neighborhood or community regeneration has crashed due to basic organizational incompetence or failure to anticipate and adapt in response to outside challenges.

At the same time, failure to address work at the upper two levels is also hazardous. The capability to work at all four levels is characteristic of life and living processes, and thus it is essential to sustainability. In order to thrive in harmony with nature, we humans must learn to integrate the work of all four levels, while holding regeneration as the overall source of guidance.

WORKING IN PLACE

The idea of *place* is a way for people to envision the unity of humans and natural systems in a concrete and specific way. In each place on Earth, natural and cultural systems express themselves uniquely (although often the qualities that differentiate them are masked by the effects of media and the global economy). This means that if we wish to engage in co-evolutionary partnerships with nature, we have to do so place by place, discovering opportunities and solutions that are indigenous to specific locations rather than generic to everywhere.

Regenerative development provides an integrated conceptual framework through which human communities can grow their shared understanding of the unique places in which they live and work. This understanding provides the armature for creating a system of sustainable design strategies and processes tailored to the unique character of a place. For example, the approaches that a North African community develops for managing its watershed will appropriately differ from those created by a city like Pittsburgh. This is not only because the soils and climates call for different engineering and biological approaches. Equally important, the local cultural and economic systems arise from different assumptions about what it means to own and steward land.

Regenerative development works on growing the capacity of the natural, cultural, and economic systems in a place. What makes this possible is the power of co-creative relationships between humans and nature. As scholars such as David Suzuki, Daniel Wildcat, Wendell Berry, and David Orr have repeatedly pointed out, it is only in relationship to place that humans experience a sense of intimacy with and responsibility for the living world. In their places, they discover meaningful identities and roles for themselves. Regenerative development returns the places where we live and those that impress themselves powerfully on our imaginations to their core position in human life. They become touchstones for shared meaning and caring that can enable people to make common cause with one another and with nature.

DEVELOPMENTAL PROCESSES

A regenerative development project leaves behind more than physical structures; it does more than benefit the surrounding natural and social communities. It also grows new capability and capacity in the people that it affects. This is accomplished by including human development in every aspect of a project.

Regenerative project teams seek to develop their capability to think and act more systemically as they engage in the work of producing designs. Local stakeholders are invited into a field of commitment and caring where they can develop understanding of their place and how it works as they step forward to serve as co-designers and ongoing stewards. Local institutions and ecosystems are seen as project beneficiaries, and it becomes an explicit project goal to improve their ability to do their work.

One example of a developmental process comes from a project that Regenesis Group participated in with the developers of Quigley Farm and Conservation Community, a proposed mixed-use ecological development in Hailey, Idaho. The developers began their planning by articulating core values for the project These emphasized a strong commitment to collaboration, transparency, and community-scale systemic change. The project team engaged the local community in a dialogue about the nature and potential of the valley they share with the farm. Rather than produce plans and ask for a response, the developers opened up the process and worked with the community to discover the role of the project in realizing the potential of its place.

This set the stage for partnership rather than adversarial positioning and allowed the developers to generate a project concept that embodied and supported the social and ecological aspirations of the community. The process was, and will continue to be, inherently developmental, enabling everyone who participates in it to think more systemically about the place where they live and the roles they could be playing within it.

None of this was accidental. It came from extending the purview of the project in order to bring about new capacity for regenerative change in a whole system. It required a truly open process on the part of the development team, one in which vision and planning were emergent, growing out of an understanding of place that came from ongoing community dialogue. Although this entailed more sophisticated thinking, it made the project inherently more strategic. In the end, the Quigley Farm team, together with the community, will accomplish far more powerful and enduring benefits than could be expected from a conventional development, at lower cost and with much less conflict.

BECOMING A REGENERATIVE PRACTITIONER

In every design project, there are three agents that powerfully influence its ability to bring about change. The first of these is the design *product*, which continues to act on the world into which it has been created. The second is the design *process*, which shapes the consciousness, capabilities, and aspirations embedded into the product. The third is the *designer*, whose unique capabilities and outlook impress themselves on everything she does. For a regenerative practitioner, each of these agents provides an opportunity to increase a project's transformative effect in the world.

A framework called "three lines of work" depicts the nature of relationships among the three agents that are required to support and sustain regenerative work (Figure B.3). Third-line work focuses on what one is trying to create in order to improve the health and value of a system (the product). Second-line work seeks to grow the capability of a community or team to work together in

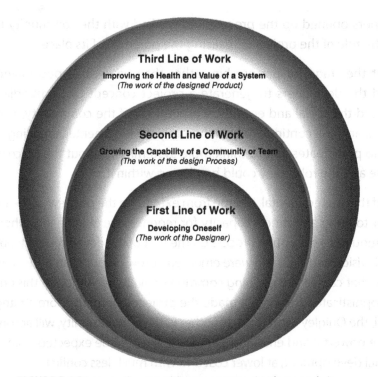

FIGURE B.3 Regenerative practitioners engage simultaneously in three lines of work.

Copyright © Regenesis Group, Inc. Illustration by Kronosphere Design

order to serve its shared third-line aim (the process). First-line work addresses the necessary growth within the individual designer that is required to make a real difference at the other two levels. A regenerative practitioner engages in all three lines of work and seeks to understand, develop, and integrate them, making them more conscious and bringing them into alignment.

Becoming a regenerative practitioner is as much about developing capability and potential in oneself and one's teams as it is about developing them in projects and communities. If humans are to be the agents of our own evolution and the enablers of the evolution we seek in the world, we must pursue all three lines of developmental work simultaneously. If we allow any one line to drop away, eventually the others will also collapse and we will become increasingly mechanical in how we think and work. This is both the challenge and the reward of taking on regenerative development.

Note

This book is organized in three parts. Part One introduces ways to think about the creation of a regenerative design *product*; Part Two addresses the regenerative design *process*; and Part Three is a brief discussion of the work that *designers* must undertake in order to practice regeneratively. Each chapter offers a core principle, illustrated by examples and case studies from around the world that guides the engagement in regenerative development practice. These principles are intended to define the parameters for a system whose creative potential has yet to be fully manifested. Readers are invited and encouraged to test them by adapting them as needed to their own situations and practices. In doing so, they will help evolve the field of regenerative development.

ENDNOTES

1. Daniel Wildcat, "Seven Things We Must Do to Advance the Rights of Mother Earth," a talk presented at the United Nation's Permanent Forum on Indigenous Issues 2012, The Indigenous Forum 2012: The Doctrine of Discovery: Its Enduring Impact on Indigenous Peoples and the Right to Redress for Past Conquests, May 7-18, 2012 (accessed March 15, 2016), www.youtube.com/watch?v=Fz25Velw6cE
2. Bradley J. Cardinale, et alia, "Biodiversity Loss and Its Impact on Humanity," *Nature*, June 7, 2012, 486(7401), pp. 59–67 (accessed March 16, 2016), www.nature.com/nature/journal/v486/n7401/full/nature11148.html
3. Millenial Ecosystem Assessment (accessed March 16, 2016), www.millenniumassessment.org/en/Condition.html.
4. Richard McClelland, Editor in Chief, Living Planet Report 2014: Species and Spaces, People and Places (Gland, Switzerland: World Wildlife Fund International , 2014), p. 6 (accessed March 16, 2016), http://assets.worldwildlife.org/publications/723/files/original/WWF-LPR2014-low_res.pdf?1413912230&_ga=1.130479752.625221973.1452275184
5. Christopher Small and Robert J. Nicholls, "A Global Analysis of Human Settlement in Coastal Zones," *Journal of Coastal Research,* Coastal Education and Research Foundation, Summer 2003, 19(3), pp. 584-599.
6. Lawrence B. Slobodkin, *Beyond Ecological Awareness* (New York: Oxford University Press, 1998).
7. Urban Sustainability Learning Group, "Staying in the Game: Exploring Options for Urban Sustainability," The Tides Foundation, June 1996 (accessed July 3, 2015), www.csu.edu/cerc/documents/StayingintheGameExploringOptionsforUrbanSustainabilityCNT-June1996.pdf
8. John Tillman Lyle, *Regenerative Design for Sustainable Development* (New York: John Wiley & Sons, 1994).
9. David Suzuki, *The Sacred Balance: Rediscovering Our Place in Nature* (Amherst: Prometheus Books, 1998).

10. United Nations, "Report of the World Commission on Environment and Development: Our Common Future" (New York: Oxford University Press, 1987).

11. Ludwig von Bertalanffy, *General System Theory: Foundations, Development, Applications* (New York: George Braziller, Inc., 1968).

12. Maria Gallucci, "Hurricane Sandy Anniversary: Five Ambitious Plans For Protecting New York City From Future Superstorms And Climate Change," IBTimes, October 28, 2014 (accessed March 16, 2016), www.ibtimes.com/hurricane-sandy-anniversary-five-ambitious-plans-protecting-new-york-city-future-1714986

13. Anne Jefferson, "Levees and the Illusion of Flood Control," Highly Allochthonous, May 19, 2011 (accessed March 16, 2016), http://all-geo.org/highlyallochthonous/2011/05/levees-and-the-illusion-of-flood-control/

14. M. Kat Anderson, *Tending the Wild: Native American Knowledge and the Management of California's Natural Resources* (Berkeley: University of California Press, 2005).

15. Ray Cole, "New Context, New Responsibilities: Building Capability," 2010 (accessed July 2, 2015), http://bookooqc.org/d1343144.html

16. Sarah Jenkin and Maibritt Pedersen Zari, *Rethinking Our Built Environments: Towards a Sustainable Future,* Research Document ME 916, (Wellington, New Zealand: Ministry for the Environment, October 2009) p. 42 (accessed March 16, 2016), www.researchgate.net/researcher/2046491969_S_Jenkin

17. Courtney White, Founding Director, Quivira Coalition (in informal conversation, April 2015).

18. Quesada Gardens Initiative, "Accomplishments," n.d. (accessed March 16, 2016), www.quesadagardens.org/resources/QGI%20Vision%20and%20Accomplishments.pdf

PART ONE

CREATING REGENERATIVE PROJECTS

Regenerative practitioners do not think about what they are designing as an end product. They think about it as the beginning of a process. Once they release it, it initiates its own process, continuing to design the world around it long after they have let it go. If designers are to contribute to a flourishing future, rather than one of diminishing prospects, how do they need to understand the world into which they unleash this unfolding process?

To do things differently, we need to see things differently.[1]

John Thackara

The Playa Viva sustainable resort and residential community is located on 200 acres adjacent to the village of Juluchuca, not far south of Zihuatanejo on the western coast of Mexico. The site includes pristine beaches, a private nature preserve, a turtle sanctuary, ancient ruins, and a natural estuary that is home to more than 200 bird species (Figure C.1).

FIGURE C.1 Private casita at Playa Viva Resort near Juluchuca, Guerrero, Mexico.
Courtesy Playa Viva copyright © Randolph Langenbach

When the project began, Juluchuca was dying. The local ecosystem had been severely degraded by monocultural oil palm plantations, subsidized by government programs in the 1920s. In recent years the palm plantations had collapsed, businesses had folded, and young people were leaving to seek opportunities in the big cities.

In a time when eco-tourism was becoming more and more popular, eco-resort developments had begun to draw criticism. While focusing on positive ecological impacts, they were inadvertently harming local communities and villages. Playa Viva has avoided this pitfall by steadfast investment in the village and its people. This has regenerated not only the ecological health of the area but also the local culture and economy.

As noted by author Laura Valdez Kurl, "Among resort projects, Playa Viva is unique in that it's focused on building relationships with the community, to learn from them, and use their knowledge to develop a better project. It's a slow process but one that demonstrates a deep commitment to the sustainability of whole communities."[2]

GROUNDED IN PLACE

David Leventhal and Sandra Kahn, Playa Viva's visionary developers and co-owners, had for a long time been committed to green building and positive community engagement. They knew that they wanted to go further with this project, to make it a regenerative force (Figure C.2). From the outset, it was apparent to them that in order to succeed, they would need to work on the vitality of the village of Juluchuca before they began building their resort.

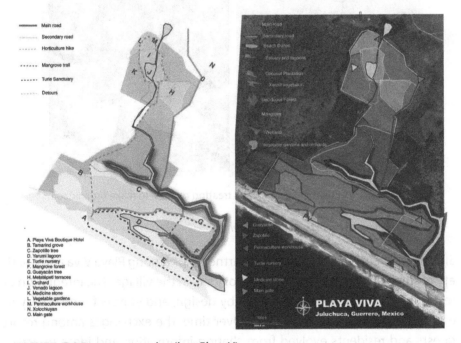

FIGURE C.2 Ecosystems and trails at Playa Viva.
Courtesy Playa Viva copyright © David Leventhal

One of their earliest efforts was to establish a training program in biodynamic growing for local farmers. This elicited a sense of cohesion, new purpose, and confidence among the participants. It also launched a partnership between the resort and the farmers, who would provide high-quality, local produce for use in its kitchen (Figure C.3).

FIGURE C.3 Local biodynamic growers treating manure to make organic soil amendments.

Courtesy Playa Viva copyright © David Leventhal

Similar programs established other partnerships among Playa Viva and a variety of small businesses and service providers in the village. The integration of resort and community was seamless by design, and visitors found it easy to establish friendships with villagers. Over time, the exchanges among resort guests and residents evolved from sharing information and ideas to actual financial investment in local businesses. The quality of life in Juluchuca was once again matched with opportunities for meaningful livelihood, and youth who had migrated away began to return (Figure C.4).

Access to the resort also reflected Leventhal and Kahn's commitment to the village. Typically, a resort wants its guests to have a special arrival experience. When looking at the options for vehicle access, the developers made a

FIGURE C.4 A vibrant local marketplace in Juluchuca.

Courtesy Playa Viva copyright © David Leventhal

conscious choice to route traffic through the village rather than build a bypass, even though this required fording a river.

At the time, Juluchuca was little more than a dispirited roadside hamlet, not a place where an eco-tourist would ordinarily choose to stop. By routing the entrance to Playa Viva through the village, Leventhal and Kahn expressed their faith in the capacity of the Juluchucans to evolve an increasingly vibrant and self-organizing community. They invested their resources and reputation in that evolution. Although recently they were forced to relocate the access road, the initial decision sent a powerful message to the village—one that Leventhal and Kahn have reinforced time and time again.

CONTINUING TO EVOLVE

Playa Viva opened in November 2009, the nadir of the Great Recession. Patterning itself on the development of biological systems, the project has allowed itself the time to adapt and expand gradually. It has become a leader in the community, with an increasingly beneficial effect on the surrounding ecosystem and its inhabitants.

In addition to providing jobs and business opportunities, Playa Viva offers workshops and training in permaculture, along with organic and biodynamic agriculture for villagers, which has enabled them to diversify and increase the value of their products. For example, local people have been positioned to respond to growing interest in organically grown coconut-based products. The polycultural systems that they have introduced into their coconut plantations have expanded the overall yields to include fruits, vegetables, and tropical flowers.

The resort has also helped develop a turtle sanctuary, initially run by volunteers, that now employs local workers (Figure C.5). Poachers who had harvested turtle eggs for the black market have now been enlisted to collect and nurture them in a hatchery, and oversee the release of baby turtles into the wild. In return, they are paid a good income and provided with ATVs to do their work. This has earned them visibility and status within the community, and they have begun to view themselves as the defenders of indigenous turtles. They have been profoundly affected by this cause and have become preservation experts, as well as significant players in the community's environmental renaissance.

FIGURE C.5 Newly hatched sea turtles find their way into the surf, with a little help from employees at the local turtle sanctuary.

Courtesy Playa Viva copyright © Daniel Camarena

Playa Viva has also sponsored a local cooperative to ensure that traditional salt harvesters receive a fair price for their product (Figure C.6). The resort sponsored a detailed chemical analysis of the salt, which revealed its unique properties and made it possible for the co-op to effectively brand it as a distinctive product from the region. Visitors to the resort who enjoy the Juluchucan salt in their food, purchase it to take home with them. In the Bay Area, former guests have actually promoted the salt to friends and local stores, helping to grow this business through person-to-person relationships rather than conventional marketing.

FIGURE C.6 A member of the salt harvesters cooperative at Juluchuca. Visitors to Playa Viva who enjoy the local salt purchase it to take home with them, and this has helped launch an export business.
Courtesy Playa Viva copyright © David Leventhal

At its core, Playa Viva was an affair of the heart and an expression of David Leventhal and Sandra Kahn's love for a place. This enabled them to uncover a rich and amazing history that had largely been forgotten. Through public education and partnership, Playa Viva has inspired members of the community to feel, rightfully, that they have a say in how their community should evolve in the future (Figure C.7).

Playa Viva was intended from the beginning to serve as a force for ongoing regeneration in its community. It is a design product that continues to act on its world in life-enhancing ways.

FIGURE C.7 A peaceful evening, poolside at Playa Viva.

Courtesy Playa Viva copyright © Randolph Langenbach

Note

The chapters that follow in Part One explore how to design this kind of effect right into a project. Each is built around a core principle that can help elevate almost any kind of project into a transformative agent. Many examples are offered of ways these principles have been applied in specific situations. It is important to note, however, that regenerative design is always based on the unique characters of particular designers, communities, and places. Rather than adopting approaches developed by others, readers are invited to invent their own ways to apply these principles to their work.

ENDNOTES

1. John Thakara, "Working with John Thakara," Doors of Perception 2015 (accessed July 2, 2015) www.doorsofperception. com/working-with-john-thackara/.
2. Laura Valdez Kurl, *Ecohabitat: Experiences in Sustainability*, quoted in "Playa Viva Resort Strengthens Local Living Economy in Mexico Community," *Green Lodging News*, February 25, 2008 (accessed August 31, 2015) www.greenlodgingnews.com/Playa-Viva-Resort-Strengthens-Local-Living-Economy-Mexico-Community.

CHAPTER 1

EVOLUTION

Can we live with a forest in a way that makes it possible for the forest to evolve? To me, that's very different from asking how to harvest the forest appropriately.[1]

Charles G. Krone

Humans often find themselves "doing battle" with nature. Lawn owners spend hours fighting weeds. Cities invest millions of dollars to manage stormwater and plow snow. Humanity puts its collective shoulder to the wheel to fight pests, control erosion, and barricade shorelines. Small wonder that these rearguard actions have turned into major economic drivers, resulting in responses as varied as the multibillion-dollar pesticide industry and the village repair shop.

We chalk up these costs—which can be energetic and political, as well as financial—to entropy, the idea that all things, even if they are maintained, will eventually deteriorate. We tell ourselves that entropy cannot be avoided.

You can plan for it, budget the time and money to counteract it, but you can't stop it.

There's just one problem with this premise. Simply put, *it is not an accurate description of the ways that living systems actually work.*

EVOLUTION VERSUS ENTROPY

Every human creation, whether it's a cottage garden powered by the sun or a company powered by employees, must function within a living planet made up of interconnected living systems. Living systems (sometimes called complex adaptive systems) are ubiquitous—hospitals, the human body, the stock market, estuaries, neighborhoods—all are living systems. Although subject to the law of entropy, living systems are also governed by the countervailing processes of evolution. Living systems don't just run down; they also grow up.

For this reason, one of the basic premises of regenerative development is that *every living system has inherent within it the possibility to move to new levels of order, differentiation, and organization.* This capacity to create increased order is the opposite of entropy.

Premise One: Every living system has inherent within it the possibility to move to new levels of order, differentiation, and organization.

Our planet is a living system, shaping and shaped by the life that it supports. This aliveness is inherently creative and unpredictable. From the beginning, this ceaseless creativity has followed a consistent pattern. Life has evolved from simple to complex, from the homogeneity of the single-celled organisms that initially colonized the planet to the myriad, highly differentiated species, microbiota to megafauna, that make up a present day Amazonian rainforest.

The evolutionary drive has been key to life's four billion years of staying power. Failure to take it into account when we design puts us in conflict with the nature of living systems and our own nature as humans. For several centuries we have strived to set ourselves apart from the unpredictable, disorderly natural world, putting our ever more powerful technologies to work making life predictable and controllable. Shaped by the Industrial Era's interpretation of evolution and natural selection as the struggle over scarce resources, we have worked to make sure we came out on top in any competition with other species.

From today's perspective, it is hard to defend this as a long-term or even short-term winning strategy. Pioneering ecologist Lawrence Slobodkin described evolution as a kind of existential game in which the only rule is to *stay in it*.[2] The implication is that, as relative newcomers to the planet, we humans need to learn how to avoid joining the 99.9 percent of species that once inhabited Earth but are now extinct.[3] For those who design and develop human habitat, the opportunity now is to redirect human activities away from the containment of life's "constant reign of evolution and perpetual novelty"[4] to collaboration with it.

Thus the first principle of regenerative development is to *design for evolution*. This represents a significant departure from the entropic ways that we've constructed our human habitat for the last four or five centuries.

Principle One: Design for evolution.

RECONCEIVING EVOLUTION

In the time since Charles Darwin published *The Origin of Species*, generations of evolutionary biologists have been refining, correcting, and adding new layers of insight as they draw on a growing body of scientific knowledge. While evolution is generally understood as a movement from simple to more complex, understanding the process through which this movement occurs is the subject of theory, research, and debate. With regard to sustainability, a particularly relevant school of thought views cooperation (deriving from the mutuality of interest among organisms and ecosystems) rather than competition as evolution's primary driver.

For more than a century, natural selection has been conceptualized as the result of a competition over scarce resources. The idea of organisms battling one another for survival still holds sway in popular culture, but current science indicates that this isn't the whole story. In the words of Martin Nowak, Director of the Program for Evolutionary Dynamics at Harvard University,

"Cooperation is needed for evolution to construct new levels of organization. The emergence of genomes, cells, multi-cellular organisms, social insects and human society are all based on cooperation."[5]

Darwin himself wrote, "The most important of all causes of organic change is . . . the mutual relation of organism to organism—the improvement of one being entailing the improvement or the extermination of others."[6] Many interpretations of Darwin's work have placed misleading emphasis on extermination over improvement of species.

Evolutionary biologist Elisabet Sahtouris has asserted that cooperation is the hallmark of a species' evolutionary trajectory. She proposes that a tendency toward competition is the marker of an immature level of biological development, occurring when a relatively new species strives to establish itself before it learns to form cooperative alliances. "Young immature species are the ones that grab as much territory and resources as they can, multiplying as fast as they can. But the process of negotiations with other species matures them, thus maturing entire ecosystems. Rainforests that have evolved over millions of years are a good example. No species is in charge—the system's leadership is distributed among all species, all knowing their part in the dance, all cooperating in mutual consistency."[7]

Sahtouris also observes that, "Multi-celled creatures are relatively huge cooperative enterprises that could never have evolved if individual cells had been doomed to struggle in scarcity."[8] For her, "The best life insurance for any species in an ecosystem is to contribute usefully to sustaining the lives of other species, a lesson we are only beginning to learn as humans."[9]

"The best life insurance for any species in an ecosystem is to contribute usefully to sustaining the lives of other species, a lesson we are only beginning to learn as humans."

—Elisabet Sahtouris

Organisms work to reproduce and survive. But the organisms that succeed in evolution are the ones that become important to the complex, multileveled larger systems they depend upon. Cooperation among organisms isn't limited to members of the same species or direct interactions among species. All organisms shape *environments* that influence other organisms.

For example, some squirrels eat the sugar-concentrated tips of spruce trees and the root-dwelling fungi that support the trees' health. In the gut of the animal, the sugars and fungal spores are brought together in the optimal conditions for spore activation. The squirrels' feces, deposited on the forest floor, carry the next generation of health-promoting fungi to the root zones of the spruce trees, and the mutualistic association continues. Every ecosystem contains examples of this kind of mutualism. It is no wonder that complexity scientist Stuart Kauffman describes the emergence and elaboration of life on our planet as, "the story not merely of evolution, but of co-evolution. We have all made our world together for almost four billion years."[10]

Even organisms that are seemingly at odds can "help" each other—not because they are altruistic, but because they play supportive roles within the ecosystem on which they mutually depend. In the Brazilian rainforest the toco toucan is the main predator of the eggs laid by the hyacinth macaw. At the same time, this macaw makes its nest in only one species of tree, whose seeds are spread almost entirely by the toco toucan.

The point is not who helps or who kills. It is that each and every organism on Earth is a *participant* in evolution. As participants, they shape not only their own destinies but the destinies of their ecosystems.

HUMAN ECOSYSTEMS

Humans have the potential to make unique contributions to the ongoing evolution of living systems by consciously participating in them. Unfortunately, for the most part we are fighting evolution rather than aligning with it. Natural systems are inherently complex, yet too often our engineering practices try to simplify them—dumbing them down, so to speak. For example, we channel, straighten, and dam rivers in order to control them for human purposes, but in the process we diminish their ability to manage themselves with regard to flooding, soil deposition, and habitat renewal (Figures 1.1 and 1.2). By treating rivers as simple conduits for delivering or removing a commodity (water), we undervalue and undermine their complex role in sustaining and elaborating life across multiple ecosystems.

FIGURE 1.1 The highly engineered drainage system of the Los Angeles River exemplifies the almost total degradation of a natural riparian system.

Copyright © trekandshoot/Shutterstock.com

FIGURE 1.2 In comparison, the drainage system of a healthy river watershed nurtures abundant and ever-evolving species in a web of complex relationships.

Copyright © Vladimir Melnikov/Shutterstock.com

Because humans are living organisms and products of evolutionary processes, we manifest the same complexity that we see in nature within our social behaviors and organizations. In the long run, the tendency toward differentiation, cooperation, altruism, and holism offer the same evolutionary advantages in human systems that they do in natural ones. Social programs intended to deliver universal access to benefits such as clean water or education create the basis for healthy, productive, and equitable societies. When such programs aim higher—for example, by seeking to realize the potential of each student rather than "teaching to the test"—they unleash the inherent capacity for holism and creativity that lies in human beings. Learning how to stay in the game, bringing human patterns into alignment with evolutionary processes, is not just a way to survive. It is also a way to prosper.

STAYING IN THE GAME

So what do we need to know about the game of evolution in order to become successful participants? How do we proactively design for evolution? Here are four fundamentals of living systems that provide some parameters for exploring this question.

The Only Constant Is Change

Living systems are marked by impermanence and change. A month of heavy rains might be followed by two months of dry weather. A bumper crop of apricots in one year might be followed by a year with a bud-killing frost. Populations of deer grow larger and larger until their predators catch up to them and thin the herds.

Designing for evolution requires us to treat change as a source of creativity. Too often, we approach projects from the mindset that change is something we are working to prevent. But this places us in conflict with living systems, trying to hold them in a state of stasis. The alternative is to harness the energies of change, as a surfer rides a wave, in order to outmaneuver the forces of entropy.

Of course, evolution not only responds to change, it also creates it. Each stage in the development of an ecosystem presents a new set of opportunities and challenges around which life must reorganize. In times of crisis (rapid and disruptive change) evolution accelerates. Explosions of new species followed each of the five mass extinctions that occurred in our planet's history. Today, ecologists are finding that species evolution is speeding up, creating new challenges for sustainable ecosystem planning. Designers who wish to work creatively with change must embrace the fact that the process is continuous. They must help build the capability to use change positively into the systems in which they are working.

Diversity Is About Exchanging Value

Surprising and unpredictable new forms emerge as the result of collective creativity. In *Complexity: The Emerging Science at the Edge of Order and Chaos*, Mitchell Waldrop wrote, "John Holland, one of the pioneers of complexity science . . . argues that organisms in an ecosystem evolve because of their interactions with one another, as an organism's ability to survive depends on what other organisms are around—'for example flowers that evolved to be fertilized by bees, and bees that evolved to live off the nectar of flowers'" (Figure 1.3).

FIGURE 1.3 The exchange of pollen and nectar is a mutualism that has driven the evolution of bees and flowers.
Copyright © Bezzangi/Shutterstock.com

A diversity of elements, such as organisms in an ecosystem or buildings on a site, adds nothing if there is no beneficial exchange of resources, energy, or material among them. A forest doesn't become healthy because it contains a long list of plant and animal species; it becomes healthy when those species actively nourish and shelter one another in an unbroken web of beneficial relationships. A downtown shopping district is more likely to foster a vibrant city economy when it is filled with local businesses that rely on local manufacturers, rather than with national chains.

A diversity of elements, such as organisms in an ecosystem or buildings on a site, adds nothing if there is no beneficial exchange of resources, energy, or material among them.

Individual elements are not key, no matter how many different kinds of them there are in a system. The diversity that matters is the network of relationships that emerges from and around interacting elements. This dynamic network is critical to evolution. In Elisabet Sahtouris's words, "The evolutionary process is an awesome improvisational dance that weaves individual, communal, ecosystemic and planetary interests into a harmonious whole."[11]

Value Enhances Viability

Exchanges become important to evolution when they create *value*. Value arises when an object or service is delivered to a recipient. It increases when, as a result, that recipient is enabled to contribute to the viability of a larger system in a continually evolving world. To return to the example of flowers and bees, when an apple blossom is pollinated by a bee, the exchange results in fruit and honey. This creates a cascade of benefits throughout the system. The bee's hive is nourished; a bear eats the apples; the apple tree reproduces itself; and the bear's scat fertilizes the soil.

In another example from the history of life's origins, early carbon dioxide–consuming microorganisms increased the level of oxygen in the atmosphere to so high a level that all life on the planet was threatened with extinction. Happily, some of those organisms developed the ability to consume oxygen and release carbon dioxide. This created the atmospheric balancing act between oxygen producers and consumers that continues to this day. These organisms, in other words, evolved the specific nature of value creation that would enable life to persist.

As living entities evolve, they upgrade the value delivered by what they produce. For example, a tree in a temperate forest builds soil by growing roots, depositing leaves, and buffering the effects of sun, wind, and precipitation. The resulting soil enables the establishment of new life. Each new organism extends and elaborates the storage capacity of the soil and thus supports the growth of the original tree. A "virtuous cycle" is brought into being, whereby the tree strengthens its community, which in turn enables the tree to grow stronger and further strengthen the community.

Adding Value Is a Nested Phenomenon

Living systems are nested. They are always part of some larger living system, and they are made up of smaller living systems. Each living system contributes to the value-adding processes of the larger system within which it is nested, and that system in turn contributes to an even larger system.

For example, a tree is a member of a larger community, called a forest. One of the outputs of an intact forest is the quality of water that it produces. The thick carpet of organic material on the forest floor quickly absorbs rainwater and then slowly releases it into springs and creeks. This contribution of the forest ripples outward in the form of river habitat and abundant estuaries (Figure 1.4).

FIGURE 1.4 In healthy natural systems, a single element such as a tree adds value to the larger systems within which it is nested.

Copyright © Regenesis Group Inc. Composited by Kronosphere Design; copyright © Inspiron.dell.vector/ Shutterstock.com; copyright © ElemenTxd/Shutterstock.com; copyright © Enre Tarimcioglue/ Shutterstock.com

If the forest is compromised or lost, then the negative effects also flow down-stream. Rainwater fails to absorb into soils and runs off too quickly into creeks and streams. This creates flooding and erosion, which degrade the aquatic habitats.

Too often, people design systems with inadequate understanding of how their effects, positive and negative, will move outward into larger and larger systems (or inward into smaller and smaller systems). As a result they create unintended consequences and fail to deliver the value of which our projects are inherently capable. For example, when small, local businesses are replaced by megastores, local money no longer absorbs into the local economy. Social interactions fostered by small businesses dry up, and the downtown may become abandoned.

Too often, people design systems with inadequate understanding of how their effects, positive and negative, will move outward into larger and larger systems (or inward into smaller and smaller systems).

REGENERATIVE GOALS

One early articulation of the role of evolution in design came from vision-ary social critic Stewart Brand. In his 1994 book, *How Buildings Learn: What Happens After They're Built*, he made the case that buildings should evolve in response to changing requirements over the long term. He believed that buildings evolve organically when their occupants refine and reshape them in response to their immediate needs. Brand called on designers to tap the inherent evolutionary power of living systems—in the case of a building, the changing community that occupies it.[12]

Brand's proposals were ahead of their time, but they were also narrow. They focused on buildings and their occupants in isolation, rather than seeing them as systems within nested and interdependent systems. The application of the principle, *design for evolution*, entails working with a complex, layered, and dynamic set of relationships. One of the first places this manifests is in *the nature of goals* that a regenerative project sets.

Projects—whether buildings, business incubators, farms, or any other organized endeavor—are undertaken to address perceived needs. Typically, they are judged to be successful based on how well they meet those needs. The success of a regenerative project is measured at another level altogether. As with Playa Viva, a regenerative project seeks to build the evolutionary capability of the systems into which it is designed—for example, organizations, communities, and watersheds.

The old adage that it's better to teach a man to fish than to give him a fish is about building capability. In the case of regenerative development, in addition to learning to fish, people learn to reestablish the inherent regenerative capacity of their fisheries, which become healthier and more productive in partnership with people (Figure 1.5). In other words, regenerative projects seek to transform human communities into *living systems enablers*. They help lay foundations for the ongoing evolution of natural and social systems, enabling them to increase in viability and health as the world changes around them.

FIGURE 1.5 Along with teaching people to fish, is it possible to teach them to regenerate the health of the fisheries on which they depend.

Copyright © Regenesis Group, Inc. Illustration by Kronosphere Design

EVOLUTION AND DESIGN

Evolution presents both challenges and opportunities for designers. It invites them to shift from working on things and structures in isolation from their context to the design of living systems with built-in evolutionary capacity. Designers who make the shift invite a far higher level of unpredictability into their work—or more accurately, they recognize the degree to which unpredictability is already present. By abandoning the illusion of control, designers enter a deeper practice, fostering the inherent creativity of the systems in which they are working.

By implication, this means that designers will need to adopt new measures of success. For example, ecologist C.S. Holling wrote that in really complex systems, wealth should be measured in the ability to evolve and adapt.[13] By this measure, the wealth or poverty of a great city might be measured by the agility or opportunism with which it addresses climate disruptions, a capability related more to the capacity for rapid and powerful collective learning than to the median income of its residents.

A regenerative approach shifts the focus of sustainable design from slowing down entropy to building the capability of living communities to evolve toward greater value. This is a much needed new role for design professionals, whose training predisposes them to manage and integrate complexity. If they accept it, designers can help correct the imbalances created by material cultures that have become divorced from natural order.

> A regenerative approach shifts the focus of sustainable design from slowing down entropy to building the capability of living communities to evolve toward greater value.

ARCHITECTURE FOR CHANGE

By now it should be apparent that an understanding of the ways that living systems evolve can be as relevant to urban design as it is to ecosystem management. The work of architect and urban theorist Teddy Cruz offers compelling examples of the application of an evolutionary point of view to the needs of impoverished communities. His project in partnership with Casa Familiar, a San Diego community development organization, is one of these.

Early in the new century, Casa Familiar and Cruz came together to pilot a new approach to neighborhood housing in San Ysidro, a border town whose median income was 60 percent lower than the rest of the county's. The result, Living Rooms at the Border, was not only conceived as a new type of affordable housing, it was designed to stimulate political, economic, and social transformation. In the years since, the project has attracted broad acclaim and was selected for the Museum of Modern Art's *MOMA 2012 Small Scale Big Change* exhibit.

Living Rooms at the Border calls for a whole new pattern of mixed-use development that is flexible enough to adapt to the changing needs of the communities it serves, even as it occupies a small, high-density site. An abandoned church located in the center of the site was repurposed as a community center and offices for Casa Familiar. A community garden and series of open-air rooms equipped with electricity and movable urban furniture enabled improvised community activities. Two buildings on either side of the church offered affordable live/work studios for artists, starter housing for young couples or single parents and children, larger houses for extended families, and accessory spaces adaptable for alternative housing as needs changed (Figure 1.6).

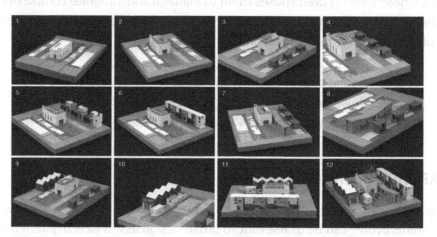

FIGURE 1.6 Teddy Cruz's renderings for Living Rooms at the Border show the project's emphasis on flexibility for the small, high-density site.

Copyright © Estudio Teddy Cruz/Living Rooms at the Border

Cruz believes that housing density needs to be understood not in terms of number of units but "in relationship to the larger infrastructure of the city, which includes transportation, ecological networks, the politics and economics of land use, and particular cultural idiosyncrasies of place."[14] He began by seeking to understand the community's living patterns. His research revealed that the formerly homogeneous suburban area had been transformed by a wide range of nonconforming, ad hoc land uses that freely mixed commercial, cultural, and residential spaces. In a workshop series called Ysidro Sin Limites, Cruz and the Casa Familiar staff met monthly with local residents to discuss their ideas of the kinds of density, interaction, spatial use, and financing that would best serve the well-being of their community.

This led the partnership to expand the project into the policy arena. It became evident that it would be necessary to identify and legalize zoning rules that would accommodate the informal negotiation of boundaries and spaces that characterized the community. This would require new stakeholder collaborations with San Diego officials. The project site was a small parcel, zoned for only three housing units. Rather than settle for a one-time rezoning, Cruz worked with the city and Casa Familiar to develop a new zoning category, the Affordable Housing Overlay Zone. This provided a framework for San Ysidro to evolve new kinds of housing and urban settlement patterns.

Cruz challenges some of the most fundamental assumptions about sustainability and sustainable communities, calling for a redefinition of density, housing, infrastructure, the role of buildings and design, and the purview and purpose of architecture itself. His practice focuses on projects that "primarily engage the micro scale of the neighborhood, transforming it into the urban laboratory of the 21st century."[15]

As inspiration, Cruz cites border towns like Tijuana, Mexico. Rather than limit himself to the characteristic architectural concerns of structure and space, Cruz studies these communities as living systems. He looks beneath their surface phenomena to see the cultural and economic exchanges by which they adaptively meet changing conditions. He has seen residents rapidly transform generic neighborhoods of identical houses into complex, layered systems of private dwellings and communal spaces. One characteristic of this evolution is the weaving of small, informal businesses throughout the fabric of the neighborhood.

Where others see poverty, Cruz sees vibrant, creative communities. This has led him to predict that, "the best ideas for the shape of cities in the future will not come from any place of economic power and abundance, but in fact from sectors of conflict and scarcity from which an urgent imagination can inspire us to rethink urban growth today."[16] At the 2009 Creative Time Summit, Cruz challenged his peers to reimagine the purpose of urban design:

> We need to redefine density, not as a series of objects thrown on the territory but as a series of exchanges. We need to negotiate a new economy and micro-politics between the top-down economics and politics of development and the bottom-up social activism of neighborhoods, creating out of these dynamics new micro-policies, micro-economies at the level of the neighborhood.... These dynamics need to redefine our tools, our practice. We as artists and architects can be the translators of [the] . . . intelligence embedded in these communities.... We can be the producers of new conceptions of citizenship and the reorganizers of resources and collaborations across jurisdictions and communities. Finally we . . . could be the designers of political processes and alternative economic frameworks.[17]

Cruz's practice illustrates the shift from design of buildings to design of systems that have the capacity to continue designing and adapting themselves. His discoveries are potentially useful to any community designer. Looked at from a regenerative perspective, they include four key ideas:

1. *Focus less on physical buildings and more on inhabitants' social flows and exchanges.* Sustainable density is not just about units per site but the number of social and economic exchanges that can occur within or flow through a site. Sustainable housing is not just affordable spaces; it is the systems of economic and cultural interactions that such spaces engender.
2. *Draw on the inherent design intelligence of the community and leave open the potential for that intelligence to source future evolution.* For development to be sustainable, it must be fundamentally inclusive.
3. *Stimulate collaborations that can engender new political processes and economic frameworks.* Designers have an important role to play as mediators between the top-down economics and politics of development and the social and creative activism of neighborhoods.

4. *Design to grow value-generating capacity*, "shifting neighborhoods from systems for consumption to producers of cultural and economic wealth." Emphasize "the construction of synergies, allowing people to move to the next level in terms of jobs and forming communities."[18]

THE BRATTLEBORO CO-OP

The first principle of regenerative development, *design for evolution*, is a reminder. It is easy to become enamored of structures—buildings, transportation networks, organizations—and their beauty. But structures are secondary. The real product of design is the work that these structures enable. For regenerative development, this work always includes the ability of people and communities to evolve to a new level of value-adding capability. In this way, regenerative projects become instruments of co-evolution in the places where they operate. (See Chapter 6 for more on value-adding.)

Here is an example that helps illustrate this point. Regenesis was asked to help the Brattleboro Food Co-op think about how to develop a new grocery store. In the process, the organization transformed its understanding of what it means to be a co-op and how to play an expanded role in the life of its community.

Formed in Brattleboro, Vermont, in 1975, the co-op started as a small buying club (Figure 1.7). Today, it occupies an entire city block, acts as an anchor business for the downtown, serves as a hub for the regional food system, promotes community accessibility to healthy local food, and supports local farmers (Figures 1.8 and 1.9). The four-story building was developed collaboratively by the co-op, the Windham and Windsor Housing Trust, and Housing Vermont. It includes a 14,580-square foot natural foods market and deli on the ground floor. The three floors above contain the co-op offices, a commissary kitchen, a cooking classroom, and 24 residential apartments on the three floors above. There are solar panels on the roof, and the entire structure uses recycled heat from the store's refrigerators. More important, the building has helped to regenerate the 6,000-member co-op's commitment to community and local food.

FIGURE 1.7 The Brattleboro Food Co-op started in 1975 as a small buying club located near the center of downtown Brattleboro.

Copyright © Brattleboro Food Co-op

FIGURE 1.8 The co-op's new building, completed in 2012, is still located near the center of downtown, where it serves as an important anchor business. Its multipurpose design supports and helps to continuously renew the 6,000-member co-op's commitment to community building and a vital local food system.

Copyright © Brattleboro Food Co-op

FIGURE 1.9 Welcome to the Brattleboro Food Co-op.

Copyright © Brattleboro Food Co-op

The transformation from buying club to regional powerhouse represents an evolution of vision and action. It began in 2002 and took nearly a decade to complete. Reflecting on the changes, Mark Goehring, the co-op's former board president said, "The most significant outcomes were the mind shifts that occurred, the changes in how we (the co-op board and management) think about things." After years of working on the co-op's internal structures and operations, "It was time to look outward. . . . No longer would the mission simply be about building and stocking a grocery store but rather taking a key role in creating a sustainable community."[19]

The co-op's growing business required new facilities. It had spent a number of years exploring its identity and articulating its values and wanted a building that reflected these. It had also explored whether to move to a new site, but had been persuaded by its members and town leaders that it had a necessary role to play in the future of downtown Brattleboro.

During these early deliberations, the co-op's board of directors became aware of the concept of regenerative development and asked Regenesis to help them think about how to shift the co-op's role from grocery store to regenerative marketplace. The ambition was to deepen their practice of their values. They knew that a green building was a start, but their vision required more. They wanted to be a positive contributor to the community and region.

Regenesis helped the board identify three changing dynamics that posed key threats to the future viability of the co-op. First, there were rumors that Whole Foods had taken note of the co-op's success and was considering opening a store in Brattleboro. Second, the co-op was vulnerable to disruption of supply lines. Like most food stores in the United States, almost all of the food on its shelves came from far away—1,500 miles on average. Third, what had once been a rich agricultural region around Brattleboro was degenerating due to depleted soils, urbanization, and an aging farmer population. The co-op was a committed community institution with deep roots in place, but also a store dependent on imported foods and vulnerable to crop failures, fuel prices, truckers' strikes, and many other external variables.

It became clear that the co-op needed a strategy to avoid displacement by a large national chain. It was also clear that the co-op needed to look beyond the task that it had initially set for itself, to build a green store (Figure 1.10).

FIGURE 1.10 A primary purpose or role of the Brattleboro Food Co-op is to support the region's farm economy and make local foods available to members.

Copyright © Brattleboro Food Co-op

The co-op developed a two-pronged strategy. First, it grounded itself in a profound awareness of place and its vanishing food heritage. It wasn't lost on the board that the energy savings that its new building might achieve would be negligible compared to the energy that could be saved by shortening the transportation distance of the food it sold. By promoting local farming and food culture through its market, the co-op could simultaneously reduce its energy footprint while making itself non-displaceable in its region.

Second, it needed to expand its conception of co-operative work to include other local organizations, businesses, and food co-ops. It set to work building a resilient business network, aligned around a shared regenerative vision of place. This opened up the possibility of considerable cost savings by sharing information, facilities, and investments in new infrastructure.

Today, the Brattleboro Food Co-op employs 100 people, and more than 60 percent of its products come from nearby farms. In partnership with local housing trusts, it provides mixed-income housing in the heart of downtown Brattleboro in an award-winning, highly energy efficient building. Indeed, the building is an energy generator and member of a local energy-generation co-op. Perhaps most significantly, it has convened an association of cooperatives and other organizations as the first stage of its 100-year plan to grow a sustainable agriculture, community, and economy for the entire region.

GUIDELINES FOR APPLYING THE PRINCIPLE

Designing *for* evolution doesn't mean designing evolution. Evolution is an emergent process—one that arises out of multiple interactions among living beings and their environments. We can't design or predict specific outcomes of evolution, but we can create evolution-friendly conditions that influence the trajectory and speed of change. The following criteria and guidelines can be used by designers to help communities steer their own evolution.

Designing *for* evolution doesn't mean designing evolution.

Maintain the potential for evolution. The designer's first task is to identify barriers to evolution. Often these are obvious, arising from attempts to control change. For example, homeowners' association rules, zoning restrictions, or building codes might have been developed for a world that no longer exists. But because they are hard to change, they continue to survive, even when they don't make much sense.

Other barriers might be less obvious. Architectural programming, a process for evaluating a client's needs and goals, has become increasingly sophisticated and inclusive. But it can be a barrier to future evolution if it perpetuates the "center out" approach, in which an individual or group designs a building for others to use.

For the Casa Familiar project, Teddy Cruz's programming process focused more on life-enhancing social flows and transformative exchanges than on physical structures. He designed buildings that were easy to modify and expand, inviting the creative engagement of both present and future users. He also engaged local government to create alternative zoning categories and new economic frameworks in order to open the door to future innovative, community-driven solutions.

Align with the wisdom of nature. Nature is a master developer. The "projects" through which the Earth structures itself—forests, meadows, reefs, estuaries—are expressions of life-generating optimum conditions for itself. Living systems structure themselves in response to their environments. By studying these systems, we can create structures that are equally responsive. For example, through understanding how a given ecosystem manages water, we gain insight into how to manage water when living within that ecosystem.

In the same way, we can pattern design solutions on the cumulative intelligence embedded in local cultures. In Tijuana, where others saw poverty and desperation, Teddy Cruz saw a vital system of micro-economies and social exchanges. Living Rooms at the Border tapped this scrappy spirit, discovering indigenous patterns rather than replicating generic, middle-class neighborhoods.

Define projects by their roles. Typically, projects are thought about in terms of the services they deliver (for example, community center, sustainable housing, water treatment). By thinking of a project in terms of its role we locate it within a systemic context. This is because a role is always played in relationship to other actors or roles and needs to be adapted to respond appropriately.

When the Brattleboro Food Co-op shifted roles from grocery store to regenerative agent, it discovered a living system of partners and allies. Not only was it able to work on its own viability; it was now a value-generating member of the entire regional community.

Grow value-generating capacity. Built structures are primarily useful because they enable value-generating activities that would be difficult or impossible without them. Unfortunately, many in the Western world, especially those who are designers, have a strong bias toward the physical. It can be hard to shift focus from the structures we want to create to the processes those structures are intended to support.

But if the intention is to work with dynamic, evolving systems, then the processes those systems use to generate value need to be the central concern: How can our projects improve the ability of everyone involved to generate more value? How can they become sources of community and economic renewal? How can the forests, meadows, and watersheds we occupy become healthier and more productive because of our presence?

From its outset, the aim of Living Rooms at the Border was to "shift neighbor-hoods from systems for consumption to producers of cultural and economic wealth."[20] It was intended to become a source of value generation for both residents of the housing development and their larger community. The proj-ect integrated socioeconomic programs to address economic, cultural, and educational needs. At the same time, flexible structures and live/work studios were designed to support the creative entrepreneurial energies of residents, offering opportunities for informal markets and shared spaces for production.

ENDNOTES

1. Charles Krone in conversation with Pamela Mang, date unrecorded.
2. Lawrence Slobodkin, "The Strategy of Evolution," *American Scientist*, 1964, 52, pp. 342–357.
3. Lawrence B. Slobodkin and Anatol Rapoport, "An Optimal Strategy of Evolution," *The Quarterly Review of Biology*, September 1974, 49(3).
4. Kevin Kelly, *Out of Control: The New Biology of Machines, Social Systems, and the Economic World* (New York: Basic Books, 1995).
5. Martin Nowak, "Five Rules for the Evolution of Cooperation,"*Science*, December 8, 2006, 314 (5805): 1560–1563.
6. Charles Darwin, *The Origin of Species* (New York: Penguin Books, 1985).
7. Elisabet Sahtouris, *Earth Dance: Living Systems in Evolution*, LifeWeb 1999 (accessed July 2, 2015), www.ratical.org/LifeWeb/Erthdnce/.
8. Elisabet Sahtouris, "The Biology of Business: New Laws of Nature Reveal a Better Way for Business," *World Business Academy, Perspectives in Business and Social Change*, 2005 19(4).
9. Elisabet Sahtouris, "Living Systems in Evolution," presented at World Parliament of Reli-gions, *At Home in the Universe: A Symposium on the Developing Dialogue between Science and Religion* (Capetown, South Africa, December 1999).
10. Stuart Kauffman, *At Home in the Universe: The Search for the Laws of Self-Organization and Complexity* (New York: Oxford University Press, 1996).
11. Elisabet Sahtouris, "The Biology of Globalization," *World Business Academy, Perspectives in Business and Social Change*, 1997, 11(3).
12. Stewart Brand, *How Buildings Learn: What Happens After They're Built* (New York: Viking Press, 1994).
13. As quoted in Joshua Cooper Ramo, *The Age of the Unthinkable: Why the New World Dis-order Constantly Surprises Us and What We Can Do About It* (New York: Little, Brown and Company, 2009).
14. Teddy Cruz, "Urban Acupuncture: A San Diego Firm Sees New Possibilities for Healing the Housing Crisis," Residential Architect: A Journal of the American Institute of Architects (accessed July 2, 2015), www.residentialarchitect.com/practice/urban-acupuncture_0.

15. "Estudio Teddy Cruz," California-architects, n.d (accessed June 29, 2015), www.california-architects.com/en/studio.

16. "Teddy Cruz: How Architectural Innovations Migrate Across Borders," TED, June 2013 (accessed June 29, 2015), www.ted.com/talks/teddy_cruz_how_architectural_innovations_migrate_across_ borders?language=en.

17. "Creative Time Summit: Teddy Cruz," YouTube, January 27, 2010 (accessed June 29, 2015), www.youtube.com/watch?v=GhKusHz9J-w.

18. Quoted at "Teddy Cruz, Architect, Estudio Teddy Cruz," Fast Company 2015 (accessed July 3, 2015), www.fastcompany.com/person/teddy-cruz.

19. Mark Goehring, "Co-op as Store Becomes Co-op as Community," Co-operative Grocer Network, March–April 2005 (accessed June 29, 2015), www.cooperativegrocer.coop/articles/2009-01-21/co-op-store-becomes-co-op-community.

20. Quoted at "Teddy Cruz, Architect, Estudio Teddy Cruz," Fast Company 2015 (accessed July 3, 2015), www.fastcompany.com/person/teddy-cruz.

CHAPTER 2

UNDERSTANDING PLACE

No one can make ecological good sense for the planet. Everyone can make ecological good sense locally, if the affection, the scale, the knowledge, the tools, and the skills are right.[1]

Wendell Berry

Green-building innovations have moved steadily from the cutting edge to acceptance as best practices for the building industry. In a similar way, sustainable community development in locations around the world has generated a parallel list of best practices. Sustainability practitioners are often asked how their approaches might offer prototypes for use in other places.

But what if this tendency toward best practices were not the solution? What if it were actually part of the problem?

■ THE COMMODIFICATION OF PLACE

On the face of it, the promulgation of good practices and ideas seems sensible. Yet adopting these practices as universal standards has the insidious effect of transforming living communities into commodities. It flattens reality, ironing out the diversity that makes the places of the world unique, interesting, and resilient.

From the beginning of the Industrial Age, communities everywhere have been losing their distinctiveness and their ability to maintain coherence and integrity as living systems. Their natural features are paved over, starved for water, and polluted. Vernacular architecture is replaced by imported styles and generic materials. Green space has been reduced to public parks, with the same swing sets, tennis courts, and ball fields that can be found in any nearby community. Local cuisine and the indigenous foods that inspire it are slowly displaced by chain restaurants and the products of industrial agriculture. The result is the development of an increasingly homogenized world in which, as James Kunstler puts it, "Every place is like no place in particular"[2] (Figure 2.1).

FIGURE 2.1 Tract housing exemplifies the replacement of distinctive cultural features with imported styles and generic materials.

Copyright © Condor 36/Shutterstock.com

It needn't be this way. In fact, no two places on the planet are the same. Local people know this. They can tell you the boundaries of their neighborhoods and point to the things that most truly reflect their authentic characters. This way of understanding place, as attenuated as it is becoming, is still alive in our human experience (Figure 2.2).

FIGURE 2.2 Historic housing in the French Quarter of New Orleans, Louisiana, expresses the cultural legacy and vibrant daily life of the neighborhood.

Copyright © Jorg Hackemann/Shutterstock.com

The special places on Earth, the ones that draw us to visit and write about them, have learned to sustain their integrity as living systems. The people who live in these places do this by celebrating and evolving their local cultures through successive generations. They adorn their buildings and streets, their clothing and food, to reflect their distinctive identities. This ongoing celebration reinforces the values that communities wish to perpetuate. It sets the norms for economic and social practices and helps harmonize them with local ecosystems. The affection we hold for these places, where the relationships among people, nature, architecture, and culture are mutually reinforcing, helps protect them from the erosive forces of globalization.

Love of place offers an antidote to the homogenization of towns, cities, and landscapes. For this reason, it is a critical piece of the sustainability puzzle because it offers the motivation needed to reintroduce regenerative practices into all of our endeavors.

This realization leads to a second basic premise of regenerative development: *Co-evolution among humans and natural systems can only be undertaken in specific places, using approaches that are precisely fitted to them.* If we wish to engage in co-evolutionary partnerships with nature, we must do so place by place, discovering opportunities and solutions that are indigenous rather than generic.

Premise Two: Co-evolution among humans and natural systems can only be undertaken in specific places, using approaches that are precisely fitted to them.

The age of industrialization has produced remarkable efficiencies in global production and consumption. But these efficiencies are mechanical rather than ecological, the result of oversimplified thinking about how nature and the world work. These efficiencies have come at the cost of rapidly degrading natural, social, and cultural wealth. John Lyle, one of the pioneers of regenerative thinking, once wrote, "Where nature evolved an ever-varying, endlessly complex network of unique places adapted to local conditions . . . humans have designed readily manageable uniformity . . . [replacing] billions of years of evolution with a simpler, more direct, and immensely powerful design of human devising."[3]

As a result, we have forgotten how to understand and live in "right relationship" to our places.[4] David Orr describes this phenomenon as becoming residents rather than inhabitants. Residency requires only cash and a map, while an inhabitant "dwells . . . in an intimate, organic, and mutually nurturing relationship with a place. Good inhabitance is an art requiring detailed knowledge of a place, the capacity for observation, and a sense of care and rootedness."[5]

Place is one of those rare concepts in the English language that embraces both the human and natural worlds. It comprises all of the multitudinous interactions among nature and culture, interactions that can be found in urban and rural settings alike. Every place is a living whole with its own distinctive spirit.

The proliferation of places, each different from any other, represents a key strategy for the planet as a living system, a diversified portfolio of investments. The innovation and experimentation that this diversity enables is necessary for the evolution of natural and cultural systems alike.

AN APPROACH TO PLACE

The ground for regenerative development is an understanding of place. What makes each place unique? What gives it vitality? Viability? What is the source of its potential and, therefore, of its capacity to evolve? With this understanding it becomes possible to tailor sustainable design strategies and processes that are harmonious with the character of a specific place. The streets of Manhattan, the vineyards of Languedoc, the wilds of the Altiplano—these are very different places and their differences demand respect and appreciation. Each expresses a unique and dynamic interplay between humans and nature that designers and community leaders can creatively harness for the benefit of all.

Regenerative development returns place to its core position in human life, making it a touchstone of shared meaning and caring that can enable people to make common cause with one another and with nature. Real communities are, in the words of David Orr, "places in which the bonds between people and those between people and the natural world create a pattern of connectedness, responsibility, and mutual need."[6]

TRANSFORMATIONAL LEVERAGE

In the context of regenerative development, the word *place* means far more than its customary usage in the fields of architecture, planning, or community development. Although it encompasses local economies and food systems, vernacular architecture, wildlife, and native plant communities, it also includes subjective experience. Place is more than material reality; for many people it is also the holder of deep emotional attachment.

For this reason, place offers a context that is meaningful to people, one that they can comprehend and care about. It is the "right scale of whole" for people to work on, providing an arena within which they can successfully take on the challenges that we are facing together as a species. Thus it represents a powerful strategic leverage point for transforming the ways we live on Earth. This is why the second principle of regenerative development is to *partner with place*.

Principle Two: Partner with place.

Place serves as the laboratory and learning environment for developing community intelligence about how to live in harmony with natural systems. Regardless of the general principles governing ecosystems, agriculture, political science, or forest and fisheries management, the particulars are always irreplaceably local. This is why, from the perspective of living harmoniously with the planet, it is such a serious loss when local or indigenous knowledge dies out. As Wendell Berry describes it:

> The loss of local culture is, in part, a practical loss and an economic one. For one thing, such a culture contains, and conveys to succeeding generations, the history of the use of the place and the knowledge of how the place may be lived in and used. For another, the pattern of reminding implies affection for the place and respect for it, and so, finally, the local culture will carry the knowledge of how the place may be well and lovingly used, and also the implicit command to use it only well and lovingly. The only true and effective "operator's manual for spaceship earth" is not a book that any human will ever write; it is hundreds of thousands of local cultures.[7]

Understanding place as a whole, encompassing all living beings, gives us an opportunity to heal our alienation. As Michael Jones has said, "A sense of place offers a unifying story that weaves together our relationship with nature, art, and community and inspires us to re-imagine, not only how we live and lead but the nature of the universe itself."[8] Scholars and philosophers like Ivan Illich, John Cameron, René Dubos, and Peter Berg have long argued that it is only in relationship to place that humans experience a sense of intimacy and responsibility with regard to the world. From this they make meaningful identities and roles for themselves.

Crucially, place is a doorway into caring. People can and do care about their places. "Rootedness in a place," wrote Simone Weil "is the most important and least recognized need of the human soul." Love of place taps into the personal and political will needed to make profound change. It can also unite people from across diverse ideological spectra because place is what all local people share. It is the commons that allows them to call themselves a community. The imperative to conserve or restore what is precious in a shared place can provide the higher-order purpose and sense of direction that reconciles a host of differences.

BECOMING PARTNERS

Partnering with place implies a relationship between living entities. We can be good stewards of the objects in our life—our house, car, clothing, etc. — using them well and maintaining them. But insofar as they are objects, we would never relate to them as partners. The first fundamental step to designing projects that can partner with place is to understand that *place is alive.*

Partnership is relational rather than transactional. In her book, *Tending the Wild*, Kat Anderson captures the indigenous worldview of the native peoples of California, who emphasize their necessary relatedness and participation with nature.

> Wilderness is a negative label for land that has not been taken care of by humans for a long time. . . . California Indians believe that when humans are gone from an area long enough, they lose the practical knowledge about correct interaction, and the plants and animals retreat spiritually from the earth or hide from humans. When intimate interaction ceases, the continuity of knowledge passed down through generations, is broken, and the land becomes "wilderness."[9]

Because partnership is relational, it moves us beyond the paternalism of protection and preservation. Conservationist Peter Forbes has noted that:

> . . . 42 percent of the private land in America is posted *No Trespassing*. And nearly 80 percent of land "protected" by private conservation organizations is posted *No Trespassing*. . . . Saving land while losing human understanding of the land, what lives there, why it needs to be part of our lives, what it has meant throughout history is to create conflict. . . . As a nation and as a movement, we've spent too much time separating

people and the land and precious little time being in dialogue about what defines a healthy relationship between the two.[10]

RENEWING THE SOURCE

The award-winning Springs Preserve in Las Vegas, Nevada, is an example of what can result when a design focus shifts from preserving to partnering. The preserve is a unique natural area located in the historic heart of Las Vegas, Nevada. It includes a Desert Living Center and Sustainability Gallery, the Nevada State Museum, Origen Museum, the University of Las Vegas DesertSol Solar House, a butterfly habitat, botanical and conservation gardens, a recreated spring pool, and extensive trails. It also houses a reservoir and pumping station that delivers potable water to much of the metropolitan area. The site is important archaeologically, historically, and culturally (Figures 2.3 and 2.4).

An abundance of sustainable and appropriate technologies integrate the preserve into the hot dry climate of the Mojave Desert. Passive solar design, rammed earth and straw bale construction, biological wastewater treatment, grid-tied photovoltaics, protection of archaeological and biological resources, and native plant landscaping have all contributed to earning it a platinum certification from the U.S. Green Building Council's LEED program. Equally important, the project is locally beloved and has become one of the city's most popular destinations. Las Vegas residents come to the preserve to learn how to incorporate water conservation and sustainable practices into their daily lives. In this way, it has positioned itself as an advocate, promoting conservation and appreciation of the desert environment as a special place to live.

The project was initially conceived as a fairly conventional demonstration site for desert gardening. A turning point came when the Las Vegas Valley Water Authority realized that it needed to shift its thinking from building a project that was *in* the desert to building one that was *of* the desert. With this shift in attitude and perspective the design team, led by the Las Vegas firm LGA, began to create something that would serve as a regenerative force.

An interdisciplinary design team that included architects, landscape architects, engineers, biologists, hydrologists, sustainability experts, and community stakeholders worked together to realize this vision. Much of the leadership

FIGURE 2.3 An architectural rendering showing the layout of botanical and conservation gardens at Springs Preserve in Las Vegas, Nevada.

Courtesy LGA

was provided by Patricia Mulroy of the Las Vegas Valley Water Authority. Before accepting a position at the Brookings Institute, Mulroy had earned a national reputation as the "Water Witch of Las Vegas." As manager of all the water resources for one of America's fastest growing cities, she demonstrated a

FIGURE 2.4 The Desert Living Center and Sustainability Gallery at Springs Preserve.
Courtesy LGA

formidable grasp of the complexities and strategic challenges raised by intense dryland development in an age of climate change. Early on, she recognized that life in a world of water scarcity was going to require more than technological solutions. It was going to require the emergence of a new culture.

Among the land holdings of Mulroy's agency was a jewel hidden in plain sight—180 acres in the heart of the city. The site housed a well field, storage tanks, and water treatment plant, and was surrounded by industrial neighborhoods. For generations it had served as a kind of open space, an unsupervised refuge for teenagers and young lovers. In the 1980s local preservationists had quietly worked with the water district to secure its historic status, but it remained dormant with regard to public engagement until the mid-1990s. The question was what to do with it.

The site contains a complex of artesian springs—a true oasis in the desert. Archaeological evidence indicates an Anasazi presence in the area, followed by the southern Paiute for whom the springs were a major water source. The Spanish encountered the lush grasslands of this oasis and gave the area its name, *Las Vegas*, which means *the meadows*. It was a major campsite on the Spanish trail, which provided an east-west link to the far-flung Spanish empire in the American southwest. In the mid-nineteenth century, the Mormons settled the area just downstream of the springs. Later, the site became an important stop on the railroad that connected Salt Lake City to Los Angeles. At the beginning of the twentieth century, developers from Los Angeles, in connection with the railroads, finally established the city of Las Vegas (Figure 2.5).

FIGURE 2.5 Botanical gardens at the Springs Preserve featuring local native plants.
Courtesy LGA

Recognizing that Las Vegas' water use was shortsighted, Mulroy knew that this project needed to catalyze a shift in the city toward a culture of sustainability. She encouraged the project team to engage in a planning process whose focus was community development rather than site development. She wanted to grow new capability within the water district, and that would require bringing together a larger than usual circle of stakeholders.

The team very quickly uncovered a profound conflict. Some wanted to preserve the site and its wealth of archeological and biological resources, while others wanted to open it to visitors and provide them with interpretation of these resources. This conflict was eventually reconciled by highlighting the historical and cultural significance of the site to the region as a whole. All parties agreed that the best way to preserve precious resources was to influence the way people live in this place.

Anchoring the project in place, making it of the desert, eventually influenced the design and building of all of its components. Every one of them was prohibited by Las Vegas' existing land use and building codes, but what was trying to come to be on the site was compelling and self-evidently appropriate. This led the various government agencies involved to adopt new codes that allowed building to go forward. Subcontractors were so proud of their participation that they would often sneak their families onto the construction site after hours. They knew that they were not just building structures; they were building community. Even before ground was broken, the project began to earn public affection and enthusiasm because it brought people into partnership with their history and ecology.

When the Springs Preserve opened its doors in 2007, its features and location attracted national attention. A visionary ecological project was so unlike the associations that most of the public have with Las Vegas—a neon playground for nightlife and high-stakes gambling—that people couldn't help but observe, "If it can happen here, it can happen anywhere!" This was one time when what happened in Las Vegas didn't need to stay in Las Vegas (Figure 2.6).

FIGURE 2.6 An aerial view of Springs Preserve in the construction phase, showing its location within the city in relation to the downtown strip.
Courtesy LGA

PLACE AS LIVING SYSTEM

Scientist and essayist René Dubos, author of the catchphrase "Think Globally, Act Locally," advocated that issues involving the environment must be addressed within their unique physical, climatic, and cultural contexts. "Each particular place," noted Dubos, "is the continuously evolving expression of a highly complex set of forces—inanimate and living—which become integrated into an organic whole."[11] In other words, places are dynamic and understanding them presents special challenges. Learning to recognize and read key patterns can greatly facilitate this work. The following three sets—patterns of nestedness, patterns of interaction, and essence patterns—are characteristic of living systems and enable insight into the uniqueness of places.

PATTERNS OF NESTEDNESS

All living systems are made of smaller systems nested within larger systems. For example, in a human body, a muscle cell is nested within a heart, which is nested within a circulatory system (Figure 2.7). All of these levels of system are whole and distinct from one another, and at the same time, they are dynamically interdependent and inseparable.

Living systems are open; they interact and co-evolve (or co-devolve) with their environments. Nestedness implies that there is a mutuality of interest among their different levels, based on the energies they exchange. Although organisms are at once complete, independent, and autonomous, they are also interdependent with other life forms.

Nature depends upon connections through different levels of biological organization. There is an unbroken continuum from cell to organism to ecosystem to bioregion and ultimately to the whole planet. "Systemic health," notes Daniel Wahl, "is a scale-linking, emergent property of healthy interactions and relationships within complex dynamic systems. The health of human beings, societies, ecosystems and the planetary life support system is fundamentally interconnected and interdependent."[12] If the health of one level of system declines, it affects the health of the other levels. A problem in the heart can adversely affect the entire body. An illness in the body can impact the health of the heart.

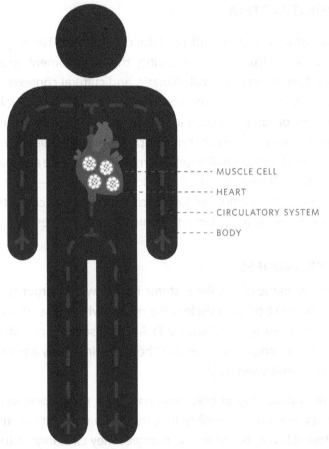

MUSCLE CELL

HEART

CIRCULATORY SYSTEM

BODY

FIGURE 2.7 Living systems are made of smaller systems nested within larger systems. Within a human body, a muscle cell is nested within a heart, which is nested within a circulatory system. (The body, in turn, is nested within a family, a larger community, and an ecosystem.)

Copyright © Regenesis Group, Inc. Illustration by David Grey and Kronosphere Design.

As living systems, places can be understood in terms of patterns of nestedness. A neighborhood or district might be nested within a city, which is nested within a watershed. As with the human body, these different levels of system are interdependent and inseparable. They don't just influence one another. They can no more exist or change independently of one another than a heart and its body can.

Many cities exhibited this dynamic interdependence following the collapse of the housing market in 2008. An abandoned house would begin to affect property prices, foreclosures would spread, and formerly healthy neighborhoods would begin to deteriorate. This would decrease income from property taxes, jeopardizing city services and further advancing the cycle of decay.

Creating a project that is regenerative requires understanding its patterns of nestedness, precisely because it is the systems within which it is nested that it will regenerate. How one defines these systems depends on what it is working on. An urban school is likely to affect its neighborhood and therefore the larger community surrounding that neighborhood. A rural school might affect several small communities located within a watershed. Each school will play a different role, based on its integration within a unique set of nested systems.

PATTERNS OF INTERACTION

Living systems are sustained by a host of interactions among diverse forces. Places, for example, are undergirded by a slowly shifting geological substrate of rocks, soils, and the spaces between them. This substrate interacts with climatic forces that wear down mountains and build up deposits of soil. Soils are further developed through their interactions with microorganisms, fungi, plants, and animals. This builds their fertility and provides a matrix for ever-increasing complexity of ecological expression, including the emergence of human habitat and culture.

These patterns of interactions can be traced backward and forward. The underlying basement of parent stone is still present even after it has been layered over with millions or even billions of years of accumulated materials. It continues to exert an influence, contributing its mineral imprint to the human communities that live above it. It helps determine the quality of the water they drink and the food they eat and, therefore, the way they live.

Virtually everything on Earth can be understood as the trace or a residue of some pattern of interaction. The Yucatan peninsula of Mexico is a great barrier reef made by living organisms, carved into its present shape by a giant meteor, riddled through with subterranean channels and caverns, overlaid by jungle and thousands of years of Mayan culture, and surging with underground rivers that surface in the form of small freshwater lakes of enormous depth. In spite of its placid surface, evidence of movement, growth, and hidden potential is everywhere.

ESSENCE PATTERNS

Essence can be defined as the true nature or distinctive character that makes something what it is; the permanent versus the accidental element of being. Architect Christopher Alexander calls it "the quality without a name . . . [the] central quality which is the root criterion of life and spirit in a man, a town, a building or a wilderness."[13] In a 2011 interview, Moshe Safde commented that, "As an architect, you have to understand the essence of a place and create a building that resonates with that."[14]

Essence can seem abstruse and esoteric until we see it at work in a family or personal context. The more deeply we understand the essence of a child, for example, the better able we are to discern the conditions in which she is likely to thrive. When an appreciation of essence informs a friendship, it enables fuller realization of each person's potential.

Places also have essences, identities, characters, and purposes. René Dubos described this phenomenon as, "spirit of place . . . the living ecological relationship between a particular location and the persons who have derived from it and added to it the various aspects of their humanness."[15] Berlin could never be mistaken for Los Angeles, and neither could be confused with Istanbul, in spite of the superficial similarities shared by urban centers everywhere. In the same way, the qualities that make the great plains of Central Asia and the great plains of North America similar, only serve to underscore their profound differences.

> Spirit has to do with essence, soul, defining attributes, life-giving principles, underlying animating structure. What gives a place its core and center of gravity? That which, if altered or taken away, would change the place fundamentally into something else. That which permeates and infuses place. What embodies place spirit? Represents or holds its essence? What stands for the physicality, materiality of place but its people and activity?[16]

Although places may appear similar on the surface, in fact each has a unique and distinct being. Until this essence becomes known, it is easily confused with superficial appearances. Italianate villas in the hills of California or half-timbered estates in Connecticut might sell well, but in those settings they are not necessarily authentic reflections of place. Edward Relph, author of the seminal work *Place and Placelessness*, condemned these inventions and manipulations as "exercises in duplicity. They are superficial acts of plagiarism that reveal a lack of confidence, a lack of originality, and uncertainty of any purpose except the one of making money."[17]

It is possible to discover the ongoing and distinctive core patterns that organize the dynamics of a given place. These core patterns are the source of its recognizable character and nature—its essence. They influence the complex relationships that produce its activities, growth, and evolution. When seeking to identify these core patterns, Regenesis asks three questions: How does this place organize and renew itself? What does it consistently pursue? What value does it generate as a result?

CREATING AN ICON

Central Park in McAllen, Texas, illustrates how discovering nestedness and essence of place can help shape a regenerative project. McAllen is a thriving, business-oriented city located in the Rio Grande estuary near the border with Mexico. City planners recently partnered with a developer to transform an abandoned, 67-acre reservoir located in the center of town next to a mixed-use park and recreational center. Conceived as a keystone in the city's effort to revitalize its urban core, the project was intended to reflect McAllen's status and direction as a regional leader. It was also intended to re-awaken a connection to the community's cultural heritage.

The city had developed a list of goals, based on the notion of a new town center that included attracting visitors, providing entertainment that would appeal to wealthy residents, and raising gross receipts tax income from high-end restaurants, stores, and events. At the same time, nearly everyone involved wanted the project to be an "icon of the future of McAllen," a reflection of its essence that would help strengthen its values and principles. Rather than simply adopting goals that could have been set by any municipality seeking to grow its economy, the developer invited Regenesis to explore the essence of place as a basis for the park's design.

DISCOVERING ESSENCE

The Regenesis team interviewed city officials, naturalists, environmental scientists and scholars, archeologists, anthropologists and cultural historians, respected elders, cultural and social activists, thought leaders, project stakeholders, and many others, all of whom had a stake in "dreaming forward" the city and region as a whole. The team members also toured the city and visited sites where characteristic ecological patterns could be observed. This yielded an overview of dynamics and history, both human and natural. Of particular interest were those places where ecological and human patterns mirrored each other.

The team was initially puzzled by the fact that McAllen's location is always officially described as the "Lower Rio Grande Valley," in spite of its location in a delta. There was no valley anywhere in the region. Then they discovered that early settlers from Mexico felt that *valley* sounded more inviting to tourists and northern investors than *delta*.

Current residents, on the other hand, describe themselves and McAllen as nested in the "Rioplex," the delta area that extends north and south of the Rio Grande and encompasses the drainage area on both sides of the border. Many feel more affinity with the Mexican city Reynosa, just a few miles from them, than they do with Brownsville, located an hour away (Figure 2.8) on the Texas side of the border. This integrative quality, which ignores the arbitrary divisions of state and national boundaries, is core to the character of this place. McAllen, the Regenesis team proposed, exhibits a "Spirit of Non-apartness."

As the research progressed, three core patterns appeared. Together they pointed to essence, as reflected in McAllen's geological, biological, and human histories. The team named these patterns "dynamic flowing," "stabilizing nets," and "living mosaic."

Dynamic flowing is how the Rioplex renews itself. Unlike a valley, which has two distinct sides, a delta is essentially a floodplain, a weave of channels and side channels, which change from season to season and year to year. In

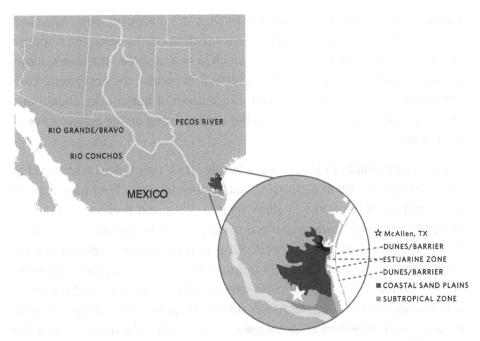

FIGURE 2.8 The location of McAllen, Texas, on the Rio Grande estuary at the Gulf of Mexico.
Copyright © Regenesis Group, Inc. Illustration by David Grey and Kronosphere Design.

the Rio Grande Delta, it is difficult to tell where the international border lies because the location of the river changes frequently. In the same way, it is hard to say where the water ends and the land begins. Monsoon rains drive periodic cycles of downstream flooding. Hurricanes drive water upstream from the Gulf.

Seasonal migrations of animals, birds, and fish cross and re-cross the landscape in pulses that mimic the water surging through this fluid terrain. These natural pulses are mirrored in the human history of the region. At times the back-and-forth flow of different human populations has influenced and even redefined McAllen's social, political, and economic landscapes. Immigrants and invasions periodically moved across the area, spreading out and interweaving with previous cultures. Like the waters of the river, each human flood left behind new resources and cultural richness, just as deposits from the floodwaters enriched the soils. This interweaving is reflected in a city where hard divides and divisiveness are antithetical to the way of life.

Stabilizing nets enable communities to thrive in this place of dynamic flows and floods. As the waters of the Rio Grande surge through the delta, the response of plant life is to form webs of roots, which slow and spread the water, allowing suspended soils and nutrients to settle and nourish the ecosystem. Even the land itself is organized in a web-like pattern of hummocks, shoals, and braiding channels, all of which together act as a brake on the erosive force of floodwater.

Human communities in and near the Rioplex have themselves responded to the pulses of change in conserving and renewing ways. They have formed stabilizing social networks to allow their cultures and livelihoods to thrive rather than be swept away in periods of war, human migration, and isolation. These adaptive, family-like connections have sustained a resilient community. Local people reported that they treasure McAllen's "slow, intimate, small hometown feel," its culture of cross-generational cooperation and traditions of volunteer activism. Even McAllen's settlement pattern is web-like, comprising a network of centers or "downtowns," each with its own unique qualities and distinctive importance.

Living mosaic is the pattern through which this place integrates diversity and creates wealth within what could otherwise be a chaotic environment. The Rioplex is an oasis, a lush multistoried jungle bounded to the north and south by deserts. It sits in one of the most biodiverse regions in the United States and contains a rich mosaic of soils that have been distributed across the landscape. Each of these soils sustains its own distinct biological community. In the same way, a diverse mosaic of cultures has formed in the area. The juxtaposition and blending of these variegated elements are the source of the variety and vibrancy of exchanges that enrich the community. When asked what truly characterizes his city, McAllen's mayor responded, "We treasure difference, diversity."

A HEALING ROLE

The Central Park developer had asked a New Urbanist design team led by Jeff Speck to conduct a five-day master planning workshop. The three core patterns were presented, and community members were asked if they were true to their experience. They responded with stories, describing the ways these patterns had played out in their own lives and the lives of their parents and grandparents. From these, the planning team extracted a set of guiding concepts.

- Welcome all ages, incomes, cultures, and languages.
- Build adaptable, well-defined spaces for a variety of uses and users.
- Make transitions between spaces gradual; avoid abrupt edges.
- Foster entrepreneurial and cultural talent.
- Reflect living water, farming heritage, ecology, and diverse cultures of the region.
- Educate and inspire; make the community's underlying values explicit.
- Integrate the global and local, the unique and the branded.

The town of McAllen has always organized itself to work like a delta, enabling exchanges among its economically and culturally diverse constituencies and visitors. Although the people of McAllen might have been expected to develop a closed, barricaded approach to these intrusions, the opposite seemed to be true. McAllen's residents liked to say, "You can get closer quicker here." The city had welcomed successive generations of newcomers into its family-like networks, creating a wealth of social capital and resilience in the face of change.

But this pattern had been disrupted on multiple fronts. The proposed border wall to separate the United States and Mexico posed significant challenges. Efforts to protect communities from flooding were upsetting the delta's ecological balance and severing the deep historical connection to the river. And the social porosity that had made the place work in the past was threatened as increasing numbers of gated communities sprang up, walling off exclusive areas from the rest of the town. Ironically, these efforts to protect the region against the dynamic flows that had shaped it were undermining its sources of renewal and regeneration.

Based on these insights, a role for the Central Park began to emerge. It needed to shed light on the underlying patterns of place and be an embodiment of the democratic exchanges that made it work. Instead of the original vision of an Epcot-like entertainment and retail center, a new design was proposed, one that would attract all segments of society, whether they had money or not. Its organizing idea was to bring people from all walks of life back into contact with water and each other (Figures 2.9 and 2.10).

FIGURE 2.9 The organizing idea for Central Park was to bring people from all walks of life into contact with water and each other.

Copyright © James Wassell/Speck & Associates LLC and DPZ Latin America

FIGURE 2.10 Water became a central element of the proposed plan.

Copyright © James Wassell/Speck & Associates LLC and DPZ Latin America

Design features included a water park, river walk, and biological water treatment system. Everything from fine dining to free water play to downtown apartments would be available, in order to encourage the mixing that was essential to the vitality of the town. By encouraging a diversity of economic and social transactions, the city would be able to achieve its high-end entertainment and tax revenue goals without undermining its core character. Not coincidentally, the pattern represented by this alternative vision for Central Park was of immediate interest to the city's powerful neighborhood associations. They could see the relevance of this planning approach as an antidote to the problem with gated communities that they were facing.

Because the project was place-sourced rather than just another trendy downtown redevelopment, it had a clear role that it could play well. As an icon for the future McAllen, it reconnected people to the rich legacy that had always been the source of strength and success for the town and its region.

GUIDELINES FOR APPLYING THE PRINCIPLE

Discovering the key patterns that can facilitate understanding a place as a living whole requires synthesizing diverse kinds of information. This work can be greatly facilitated by three somewhat unusual questions. *"How big is here?"* looks at place through the lens of nested systems. *"How does here work?"* relates to patterns of interaction. *"What kind of here is this?"* brings in the aspect of essence.

HOW BIG IS HERE?

It can be tricky to find the right nested systems for a project. One needs to identify the appropriate scale within which it can have a meaningful influence. As a starting point, Regenesis uses a relatively simple framework that shows three levels (Figure 2.11).

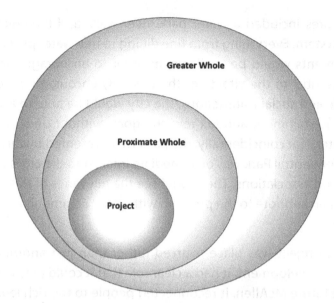

FIGURE 2.11 Every project is nested within its place (its proximate whole), which is nested within a greater whole.

Copyright © Regenesis Group, Inc. Illustration by David Grey and Kronosphere Design

In the framework, the inner ring represents the project, which could be as limited as a single building or piece of infrastructure or as large as a regional planning effort.

The next ring is the *proximate whole*. This is a living system in close relationship to the project, one that is coherent and bounded by natural features of the landscape and/or cultural agreement. It is usually possible to see direct effects and exchanges between the project and its proximate whole or to imagine them occurring in the future. Some examples are the neighborhood in which a building is sited or the watershed within which a township is located.

The third ring, or *greater whole*, is the next higher level of system, within which the proximate whole plays a role. If the project is a building, and a neighborhood is the proximate whole, then the district or city is the greater whole.

Humans draw boundaries to define and give form to whatever they wish to work on. This makes it possible to navigate in a world where "everything is connected to everything." However, it is important to hold in mind Buckminster

Fuller's reported admonition that "every boundary is a useful bit of fiction." Identifying boundaries to define a project's nested wholes is a process of discernment; a series of refinements that will change as understanding grows and deepens.

HOW DOES HERE WORK?

Part of the art and discipline of holistic thinking is the ability to scan disciplines and sources of information in order to bring them together in a way that generates meaning. This is sometimes referred to as pattern literacy. It is the ability to see the underlying patterns that link and make sense of disparate forms of information.

For example, looking at political or economic boundaries rarely reveals how a living system actually works. Looking at place from a pattern perspective yields a very different picture.

Patterns of Geophysical Organizing

Looking at how the physical landscape is structured often provides clues about the dynamic operations that are at work in a place. For example, the Rio Grande has been structuring the delta where McAllen, Texas, is located for thousands of years, and this has exerted a subtle but pervasive influence on the region. Even landscapes that have been radically altered by humans, such as densely populated urban centers, continue to be shaped by geophysical organizing.

Patterns of Biological Organizing

Biological systems (for example, a forest ecosystem) generally organize themselves to moderate or take advantage of underlying geophysical conditions (although, of course, this process can be disrupted by human interventions). Interactions among climate, soils, and hydrology shape local biological communities. To learn more about this aspect of a place, it can be useful to seek out an ecological history. This can provide a sense of the ways these communities have responded to changing conditions.

Patterns of Human Organizing

Place-sourced human culture arises in response to geophysical and biological organization. For example, whether a landscape is forested or open, coastal or mountainous, will have a profound influence on how people provide for themselves, shelter themselves, and transact with each other and the world at large. At the same time, humans also contribute to making places what they are.

WHAT KIND OF HERE IS THIS?

Regenerative development gains much of its power from the ability of design practitioners to discern the essences of places by observing and engaging with the people who live in them. Here are three different approaches to this delicate work. They are a good way to begin, but they are by no means an exhaustive list.

How Do Local People Describe Place?

Though we may not be aware of it, we often talk and think about the places where we live in a nested way. If someone asks us where we live, we might answer with the name of the state or region. Pressed for more details, we would name our city or district or neighborhood or street. Depending on our shared level of local knowledge, we might offer landmarks ("across the river") or even historical references ("next to where the grocery store used to be, before it burned down"). This layered approach is commonly used to contextualize all kinds of relationships.

Locational definitions are often reflected in the way newspapers or television broadcasts characterize their areas: serving "the tri-county area" or "the upper valley." Local people know exactly what these phrases mean, along with a host of others that capture the larger and smaller contexts of place. One can begin to develop an understanding of a place and a sense of the boundaries between proximate and greater wholes by inviting local people to share how they think about where they live.

How Do Local People Express Place?

A highly informative way to gain insight about the character of place is to notice how people celebrate it. This can take the form of fairs or parades or community days. It can be reflected in the way people spruce up their streets, especially when the sprucing is done by neighborhood residents rather than government agencies or business boosters. These are indicators of what people take pride in and how they express it. The task is to see through what is presented externally to the message behind it.

Clues to the essence of a place can be found in all kinds of interesting sources. Very often, even small communities will have a cookbook of local recipes. Along with local variations on regional cuisines and foodstuffs, these can offer glimpses into local lives and histories. Some communities are lucky enough to have published oral histories, which not only flesh out the understanding of past events and local mores, but also allow the reader to discern the inflection and the spirit of residents. Local literature and art can also be rich sources of insight. Novels, paintings, and music that successfully capture feelings and values of residents can provide windows into the lived experience of place that data simply doesn't offer.

What Do Local People Love about Their Place?

Almost all conversations with people about the places where they live ultimately lead back to the heart of the matter, which is why they live there in the first place. What is it that they love? What is it that they want other people to experience because it is so dear to them? When people get in touch with the genuine affection and caring they feel for their places, they enable others to contact the deeper, inner realities at work in them. Often these deeper sources of caring are diminished or even forgotten in the course of day-to-day living. Eliciting from people what they love about where they live not only reveals its essence; it regenerates their sense of connection to it.

ENDNOTES

1. Wendell Berry, "Out of Your Car, Off Your Horse: Twenty-Seven Propositions about Global Thinking and the Sustainability of Cities," The Atlantic (accessed August 20, 2015), www.theatlantic.com/magazine/archive/1991/02/out-your-car-your-horse/309159/
2. James Howard Kunstler, *The Geography of Nowhere: The Rise and Decline of America's Man-Made Landscape* (New York: Touchstone, 1994).
3. John Tillman Lyle, *Design for Human Ecosystems: Landscape, Land Use, and Natural Resources* (New York: Van Nostrand Reinhold, 1985).
4. Aldo Leopold, *A Sand County Almanac* (New York: Oxford University Press, 1949), p. 262. To paraphrase Leopold, "right relationship" is used here in the sense of "A thing is right when it tends to preserve [and evolve] the integrity, stability and beauty of the biotic community [all of life]. It is wrong when it tends otherwise."

5. David W. Orr, *Ecological Literacy: Education and the Transition to a Postmodern World* (Albany: State University of New York Press, 1991).

6. David W. Orr, *Earth in Mind: On Education, Environment, and the Human Prospect* (Washington, DC: Island Press, 2004).

7. Wendell Berry, *What Are People For?* (Berkeley: Counterpoint Press, 1990, 2010).

8. Michael Jones, *The Soul of Place: Re-imagining Leadership Through Nature, Art and Community* (Victoria, British Columbia: Friesen Press, 2014).

9. M. Kat Anderson, *Tending the Wild: Native American Knowledge and the Management of California's Natural Resources* (Berkeley: University of California Press, 2005).

10. Peter Forbes, "What Is a Whole Community? And Why Should We Care?" Center for Whole Communities, 2006 (accessed August 31, 2015), www.wholecommunities.org/pdf/publications/What%20is%20a%20Whole%20Community.pdf.

11. René Dubos, *A God Within: A Positive Approach to Man's Future as Part of the Natural World* (New York: Macmillan Publishing Co., 1972).

12. D. C. Wahl, "Management of Natural Resources, Sustainable Development, and Ecological Hazards," *WIT Transactions on Ecology and the Environment,* Vol 99, 2009.

13. Christopher Alexander, *The Timeless Way of Building* (New York: Oxford University Press, 1979).

14. Moshe Safde, PBS Newshour, October 14, 2011.

15. Ibid.

16. Tim White, "Travel Drawing: Engaging the Spirit of Place," *Environmental and Architectural Phenomenology*, 14/3, Winter 2003 (Accessed August 14, 2015), www.academia.edu/4010375/ENVIRONMENTAL_and_ARCHITECTURAL_PHENOMENOLOGY_vol_14_2003_3_issues.

17. Edward Relph, "Reflections on Place and Placelessness," Environmental & Architectural Phenomenolgy Newsletter 1996 7(3).

CHAPTER 3

DISCOVERING
COLLECTIVE VOCATION

Where your talents and the needs of the world cross,
there lies your vocation.

Attributed to Aristotle

When a community awakens to its uniqueness, it taps into a potency that comes from operating authentically, from the core of who it is. This potency can be drained away by conventional planning efforts, which tend to destroy wholeness by breaking problems into their component parts in order to solve them. This is as true of sustainability planning, with its model projects and rating systems, as it is of economic development efforts or infrastructure overhauls. Most of the time, these efforts fail to pay sufficient attention to the living systems in which the parts are embedded.

Improving the many parts and pieces that make up a complex modern community is a good thing. However, focusing solely at the level of individual elements is fundamentally incompatible with the way nature works. For example, from a living systems perspective, a sustainable building is a meaningless idea. The point is not to sustain buildings; the point is to make beneficial contributions to the future of life on Earth.

How does one begin to shift collective attention from mechanical parts to living wholes? From piecemeal solutions to system regeneration? From best practices to authentic, place-sourced creativity?

SUSTAINABILITY IS A BYPRODUCT

Sustainability is actually a byproduct of growing the value that living systems create. Sustainability becomes possible when a person, forest, or river is in a reciprocally developmental relationship with the proximate whole it inhabits. The smaller system contributes to the larger system's development and, in turn, receives nourishment for its own. This relationship is described as "adding value."

The premise that arises from this insight may be stated as: *the sustainability of a living system is tied directly to its beneficial integration into a larger system*. For humans, the desire to contribute to something larger is inherent and may be a trait that has allowed us to co-evolve with our planet and with one another. This contribution doesn't just make life more meaningful; it is also the only path to a sustainable way of living. One of the implications of this idea is that, in order to be regenerative, one must develop the ability to *take direction* from a higher-level system.

Premise Three: The sustainability of a living system is tied directly to its beneficial integration into a larger system.

THE IDEA OF VOCATION

In regenerative development, taking direction does not mean taking orders or following instructions. Rather, it is a pulling or a calling forth, in other words, a *vocation*. Vocation is the trail to which a person is especially drawn because she knows that it is hers to blaze. Every member of a living system is known, in part, by the contribution to which it is called.

For human beings, vocation is a source of meaning. When a person responds to a calling, her life is enriched by a sense of direction. This is true for not only individuals, but also their communities and places. Smaller systems gain meaning from the beneficial contributions that larger systems call forth from them.

Within human communities, a collective vocation enables people to work intentionally, independently, and in diverse ways toward a common aim. Put another way, a collective vocation provides a context within which people are able to discover their individual vocations. By eliciting a collective vocation, a regenerative project can help a community coalesce around its shared purpose, inspiring will and action, and illuminating a path to sustainability suited to the unique character of a place.

Jaime Lerner, the renowned former mayor of Curitiba, Brazil, has said that every great city has a vocation. This visionary calling is the means by which a city makes its distinctive, significant contribution to the world. Like an individual's vocation, a vocation of place can be seen as an expression of essence in the form of new life that will allow both the place and its world to evolve.

> Like an individual's vocation, a vocation of place can be seen as an expression of essence in the form of new life that will allow both the place and its world to evolve.

For example, a degraded watershed is calling to be restored to health. When a community accepts this responsibility, it organizes its talents and resources to restore not only the watershed's hydrological function but its unique—and, for some people, sacred—place in the order of things. This action and the challenges it presents have the potential to regenerate not only the watershed, but the community as well, renewing its life and sense of collective identity. In this way, the watershed and community are engaged in a reciprocally developmental relationship that increases the vitality and viability of both. This pattern of mutuality informs all truly regenerative projects.

Thus, the third principle of regenerative development is to *call forth a collective vocation*.

Principle Three: Call forth a collective vocation.

CURITIBA

Curitiba, a provincial capital of approximately 2.5 million people, is located in southeastern Brazil[1] (Figure 3.1). It has no exceptional landmarks, no beaches or vistas, and it rains a lot. In the last century, large numbers of migrants began arriving from the surrounding countryside, slums and shanty towns sprang up around the city's edges, and resources dwindled. Yet, rather than succumb to poverty, unemployment, inequity, and pollution, Curitiba's citizens have brought about continuous improvement in their quality of life.

FIGURE 3.1 Aerial view of Curitiba, Brazil.
Copyright © Tupungato/Shutterstock.com

In fact, Curitiba is regularly held up as one of the world's leading models for ecological urban development and planning. The statistics show why:

- The amount of green space per capita in the city has risen in the past 30 years from a dismal half square meter per inhabitant to more than 50 square meters. Nearly one-fifth of the city is now parkland.
- Volunteers have planted more than 1.5 million trees along streets and avenues.
- Curitiba's fast and efficient bus system carries more passengers per weekday than New York City's and runs with an 89 percent approval rating.
- Auto traffic has declined by more than 30 percent since 1974, even though the city's population doubled during that time and there are more car owners per capita in Curitiba than anywhere else in Brazil.
- A larger percentage of people in Curitiba recycle than anywhere else in the world. As much as 70 percent of the city's trash is now recycled.
- Curitiba's 30-year economic growth rate was 7.1 percent higher than the national average, resulting in a per capita income that is now 66 percent higher than the Brazilian average.[2]

What makes these accomplishments even more impressive is that they have been accomplished despite a severely limited civic budget. Many of Curitiba's programs are designed to help pay for themselves, address multiple civic issues at once, and enable the work of other programs.

Civic spirit and pride has risen dramatically during the last 50 years. In surveys conducted in the 1990s, more than 99 percent of Curitibans told pollsters that, if they could choose to live anywhere in the world, they would stay in Curitiba. In similar polls conducted in New York City, 60 percent said they would rather live somewhere else. In Sao Paulo, 70 percent said they would rather live in Curitiba.[3]

Much of this transformation can be attributed to the leadership of Jaime Lerner and his core development team, who have been particularly articulate about the need for a collective vocation. It starts, Lerner observed, "from knowing and loving your village—interpreting its collective dream."[4] In the years before 1970, when Lerner was elected mayor, he and his associates in the architecture and planning departments of the local branch of the federal university would gather mornings at a local coffee house. Their conversations centered on the city they had grown up in and loved, and their vision of what it could become.

After he was elected, Lerner continued this practice of visioning Curitiba's future. His team's living-systems approach helped Curitiba successfully integrate the powerful forces of change that were devastating urban centers in developing nations around the world. Every morning, they would meet in a log cabin retreat in the middle of a forested city park, where they worked only "on what [was] fundamental, on what would affect a large number of people and could create change for the better." In the afternoon, they would return to city hall to meet with their constituents and to deal with the city's day-to-day needs.[5]

SCHOOL OF ECOLOGICAL URBANISM

Out of this daily interweaving of large-scale planning and engagement with the needs and hopes of the people, a vision emerged of a city whose vocation was to function as a *school of ecological urbanism*. Drawing from the theme of ecological urbanism, the team began to develop a set of guidelines for their engagement with the community, which would shape the myriad creative solutions through which Curitiba has developed itself over the last 40 years.[6]

One of the team's core beliefs was that *the city is a living system*. "The city is an organic entity, and as such it imitates nature."[7] Curitiba "is an organic whole. Public administration is compelled to understand this and to go along with its natural evolution."[8] According to Lerner, "Every city has its hidden designs—old roads, old streetcar ways. You're not going to invent a new city. Instead, you're doing a strange archeology, trying to enhance the old, hidden design."[9]

In Curitiba, this "strange archeology" required understanding more than just historical settlement patterns. It also extended to local ecosystems. Curitiba lies on a forested flood plain where multiple rivers intersect and the greatest diversity of life is concentrated along the river corridors. When humans settled the plain, first as indigenous peoples and later as European and other immigrant groups, they set up transportation corridors that ran alongside and tended to mirror the river corridors. This flow of commerce and human exchange matched the flow of biological exchange and led to the development of many of the major roads that run through Curitiba today.

These patterns led Lerner and his core team to the realization that the traditional radial model of cities—a densely populated center surrounded by increasingly less dense areas—did not match the way life worked in Curitiba. From this, they developed the core concept of "linear city with structural arteries," with concentration of commercial and residential use along the major corridors of transportation. The tallest buildings, the majority of commercial activity, and the greatest intensity of public transportation routes occur along these corridors, which makes Curitiba's groundbreaking transit system both effective and affordable. At the same time, the lands around the biological corridors (the rivers and riparian systems) were purchased by the city and developed into linear parks, running parallel along the densely populated urban transportation corridors. As one leader put it, this helped to "keep the rivers flowing naturally"[10] (Figures 3.2 and 3.3).

FIGURE 3.2 Lands around Curitiba's rivers and riparian systems were purchased by the city and developed into linear parks, running parallel along densely populated urban transportation corridors.

Copyright © Paulo Marcel Coelho Aragão/flickr.com Creative Commons

FIGURE 3.3 Curitiba Botanical Garden is also located in a densely populated area within the city.

Copyright © Hugo Brizard/Shutterstock.com

LEVERAGING WILL

In addition to orienting the work of the planning team, Curitiba's vocation as a school of ecological urbanism provided the basis for creating solidarity among its citizens and political will to take on ever larger challenges. The team emphasized the importance of taking human well-being into account while considering environmental responsibility. "Man is not merely an observer of nature. He is a part of nature. All environmental actions must take him into account." At the same time, "The zeal for ecological legacy is not just the concern of public powers. On the contrary, it is a whole community's task."[11]

Programs and projects were developed in partnership with citizens as a way to create what city leaders called an "equation of co-responsibility."[12] As Cassio Taniguchi, another of the city's mayors, put it, "No matter how well run we are, we still would not have all the resources we need. We can only get those resources by mobilizing more people to participate and take co-responsibility for devising solutions."[13]

Every major initiative undertaken by the city engaged key stakeholders (both public and private) in dialogues to find co-responsible solutions.[14] In one particularly famous example, the city was faced with an emerging public health crisis. There were no streets in the informal settlements, or *favelas*, that were sprouting up around the city, and city workers couldn't get in to remove garbage. Lerner's team proposed to residents that, in exchange for trash, they would receive tokens that could be used to buy produce in the local farmers markets or rides on public transit. The program was wildly successful. Not only did it address the immediate trash problem, it also provided the city's poorest citizens with access to nutritious food and transportation. In addition, it helped underwrite local agriculture. It did all this in a way that showed respect for the self-organizing capacity of *favela* residents.

All over the world, people dream up ecologically inspired ideas every day, but very few communities have the political will to carry them out. In Curitiba, the significance of innovation wasn't the ideas themselves. It was the process through which they emerged slowly and consistently as coherent responses to the city's collective vocation. As this vocation became embedded in the culture of the city, innovations bubbled up from multiple sources within city government and the community at large, becoming the basis for creative partnering.

> As Curitiba's vocation became embedded in the culture of the city, innovations bubbled up from multiple sources within city government and the community at large, becoming the basis for creative partnering

SOURCING DIRECTION

Vocations orient decision makers and provide guidance for action. As such, they are sources of *direction*. Every design project, and in fact every complex activity, is guided by a set of values or principles (often unconscious) that keep it headed in its intended direction.

The choice of direction has consequences that can be seen all around us. For example, *infinite diversity* is the direction that guides nature's design processes. Yet, for more than a century, *manageable uniformity* has guided the design of human communities. Referring to the often degenerative consequences of manageable uniformity, Aldo Leopold wrote, "We are remodeling the Alhambra with a steam-shovel, and we are proud of our yardage."[15]

Maximum yield, another example of direction, has had devastating impacts. For example, fisheries have long been managed by setting maximum catches for individual species, while ignoring the complex interdependent dynamics of ocean ecosystems. In contrast, Ecosystem-Based Fishery Management is guided by *optimal yield*, a more holistic source of direction that emphasizes the biodiversity required to sustain the health of every level of ecosystem, from small niches to large ocean regions. Its decisions are based on emerging information about the interplay of social and ecological systems.

Manageable uniformity and maximum yield arise from mechanistic thinking. They assume that the world is composed of separate parts that can be studied, manipulated, and managed in isolated and linear ways. As sources of direction they almost always lead to actions that conflict with the working of complex ecological and social systems.

On the other hand, infinite diversity and optimal yield take into account the ways that species and ecosystems are embedded within and interdependent upon each other and how this shapes the dynamics of evolution. As sources of direction, they require accountability for the consequences of actions across systems and through time. Thus, they enable projects to produce *wealth*— defined as the conditions for well-being—for the integrated whole of the systems within which they work.

VOCATION OF PLACE

A regenerative project takes direction from the vocation of its place. This is because it seeks to remain present and relevant—continually influencing the evolution of larger systems—long beyond its design and implementation phases.

Vocation of place provides direction for everyone in the community, including the project team, and therefore it is the basis for enduring, co-creative partnerships. A project guided by this vocation is capable of aligning its activities with what is needed by the nested systems it serves, and thus it may become a perpetual contributor to their vitality and viability.

Perhaps most important, vocation of place enables the integration of two processes that are essential to all regenerative projects: *organizing* with *ordering*.

ORGANIZING

Organizing has to do with bringing activities and materials together in ways that are effective and efficient. It enables a project to stay on track, meet benchmarks, and use time and resources well. When people are organized, they know where they're going and why.

Organizing a project around vocation of place provides it with a polestar that helps make choices practical, consistent, coherent, and in harmony with the systems that the project is serving. A vocation maintains the integrity of work and keeps the project connected to the living, dynamic processes that it is trying to produce in its place.

For example, working to become a school of ecological urbanism enabled the Curitiba team to discern which actions were most likely to manifest a vibrant future for their city. Jaime Lerner often speaks of the importance of moving quickly, which produced powerful results in Curitiba. But in other times and places, quick action has had the opposite effect. What made the difference in Curitiba was using vocation of place to provide a context for organizing work. This ensured that quick actions were also systemically beneficial.

Still, however connected organizing is to vocation of place, it cannot enable regeneration by itself. It doesn't call people to elevate their capability or reimagine how they work. In an evolving world, a project that aspires to deliver only the same level of excellence and value that it started from is caught with Alice in the Red Queen's dilemma, "here we must run as fast as we can, just to stay in place. And if you wish to go anywhere you must run twice as fast as that."[16]

ORDERING

In addition to organizing how we work, vocation must be a source for *ordering*, moving work up to higher levels. A regenerative project aims to elicit new expressions of essence. As it works to realize its place's potential, it also grows the value-generating capability of those who carry it out.

Vocation of place provides a touchstone that helps people sustain a connection to the deeper meaning and significance of their work. It evokes new spirit and inspires people to be the best they can be as they work. It invites higher levels of consciousness and creativity, and offers opportunities for personal transformation. In the midst of deadlines, benchmarks, budgets, and schedules, recalling vocation of place keeps people connected to what they most care about.

NESTED VOCATIONS

With a compelling, collective vocation, a community becomes capable of inspiring its members to take on collaborative and integrative efforts. This is the development of *nested vocations*, where individual vocations become aligned with larger, shared vocations.

For example, Curitiba's taxi drivers strongly opposed plans to revolutionize the city's public transit system. But when they were invited into a dialogue with planners about the city's vocation and future, they were able to identify an entirely new role for themselves. Rather than see themselves as transportation providers, they began to envision themselves as docents, interpreting the accomplishments that made their city unique. They became knowledgeable tour guides, offering residents and visitors insight into the evolving life of the community. This enabled them to flourish as an industry while becoming champions for Curitiba's visionary aspirations.

As nested vocations become increasingly conscious and aligned, they reconcile the apparent conflict between thinking globally and working locally.

Stakeholders look beyond their work to see its effect in their socioecological communities. Communities begin to realize new potential through the roles they play within larger, bioregional systems. Regional identities are reframed around the unique value that they bring to the global community.

In making vocation of place their sources of direction, projects also take on new significance and meaning. This enables project team members to explore their own vocations and discover ways that their personal potential can contribute to the places where they live and work.

GIVING VOICE TO VOCATION

The first challenge to tapping the power of vocation is eliciting or uncovering it. Unlike Curitiba, few communities are aware enough of their vocation to speak about it. The following describes how one designer helped make vocation of place explicit.

LA PALMILLA

Architect Raul de Villafranca approached the Regenesis team for help in thinking about El Jobo, his mixed-use development project in the Rio Bobos watershed of Veracruz, Mexico. Villafranca is a leader in the Latin American biomimicry community, where he is known as a practitioner who applies biologically derived principles to design. On this project he was also a co-developer. He was committed to working exclusively from regenerative principles because he cared passionately about the community and had dedicated much of his professional life to protecting the watershed.

El Jobo lies near the river in an area called La Palmilla, nested in a region rich in history, natural and cultural diversity, and tradition. This is the northern limit of Latin America's tropical forests and the place of origin for the orchid whose seedpod is the vanilla bean. Nearby villages are known for their unique local foods, although the land now mostly lies fallow due to the economic pressures of globalization (Figure 3.4).

FIGURE 3.4 La Palmilla, an area of the Rio Bobos watershed of Veracruz, Mexico.

Copyright © Raul Villafranca

Villafranca held a vision of what La Palmilla could become, given its heritage and biodiversity. He wanted to catalyze an agroforestry economy as the basis for a sustainable watershed culture. The system he proposed would integrate wild, native plants with traditionally cultivated ones. He talked with Regenesis about reestablishing local food crops and artisanal products for local use. In addition, an export economy would focus on crops that represent the distinctive character of the place (high-quality vanilla beans, for example). Agricultural and ecological tourism would be included in the mix, as well as housing for urban refugees seeking a more peaceful rural life.

Villafranca argued that to increase vitality in the region would require creating livelihoods that local people could take pride in. Growing its viability would require a functioning economic system based on non-displaceable products and services. The region's capacity for evolution would be increased by integrating its economy across multiple industries—for example, ecotourism, agriculture, research, and education (Figure 3.5).

FIGURE 3.5 Recently discovered ruins in La Palmilla, partially excavated and developed for tourism.

Copyright © Raul Villafranca

Villafranca imagined a residential community within a productive agroforestry landscape. An on-site nursery would supply local farmers with the plants needed to create their own agroforests; a farm would demonstrate the economic validity of the concept; and a boutique hotel would feature local foods and crafts. As part of its overall strategy, the project would support the reestablishment of a *mercado* in the adjoining village. Villafranca's concept was to showcase local culture and products in a way that enabled local people to see the true value in what they had—a strategy very similar to the one pursued by Italy's slow food movement.

PEOPLE AND PLACE, WOVEN TOGETHER

Villafranca's vision clearly called for something more than the standard design and development process. The project needed to connect to a vocation for La Pamilla that would inspire key stakeholders to get involved and invite them to step up to new and creative ways of working together.

For almost a thousand years the region's culture had sustained a relationship of respect and caring between humans and nature, and both had thrived. However, over the last century the culture had steadily deteriorated under the forces of modernization and industry. Still, the sense of place held deep resonance for local people. Reawakened, it would be a powerful source of coalescence. Based on this, Villafranca intuited that Palmilla's vocation was *reweaving people with place*.

He tested this statement to develop a sense of its likely effect. He could see that evoking this vocation would help the project team remember to direct its efforts at more than just inventing an agroforestry industry. Their work must also support the seamless integration of people and nature. Without a clearly articulated statement of vocation, he acknowledged, it would be all too easy to become sidetracked, chasing financial profits that made no contribution to furthering the goal of integration (Figure 3.6).

el jobo
plan maestro   fase conceptual

FIGURE 3.6 The El Jobo project master plan, developed in the conceptual phase.
Copyright © Raul Villafranca

GUIDELINES FOR APPLYING THE PRINCIPLE

Ideally, a statement of vocation flows from an integrative process that engages people with the unique potential of their place and what it is called to become. As images emerge, intuiting a statement of vocation requires openness and sensitivity and the elimination of attachment to preexisting ideas.

Some communities discover their vocation when they attempt to brand themselves. But when branding is used indiscriminately (for example, to attract tourism and new industries that have no relationship with the essence of a place), it can have unanticipated side effects. For example, in 1990, Glasgow, Scotland, sought and was awarded the title "European Capital of Culture." The city launched the campaign to win the title with the aim of revitalizing its economically depressed region. But when it used the title to hide its working-class heritage and socialist history, it evoked resentment and hostility. Many residents felt that their contributions were devalued or dismissed.[17]

When discovery of vocation is approached with humility and appreciation, as an exercise in deep listening, it is a powerful opportunity to begin coalescing will among different stakeholders. If the experience begins to feel arduous or unwieldy, people have probably dropped out of the process and are trying to think vocation into existence.

DISCOVERING VOCATION

Eliciting vocation of place is an iterative process that requires both reflective dialogue and research. Because every place is unique, there is no one right way to discover vocation. Below are four distinct but complementary approaches that can help to reveal the vocation of a place.

See a trajectory. One way to begin the process is by imagining a place within a stream of time. What value is this place continually working to create for its region—and for its watershed, nation, and the world? What would a higher expression of that value look like? What changes would need to occur to make it possible to pursue this higher expression?

For El Jobo, vocation of place first emerged from seeing the relationship of caring between humans and nature that made La Palmilla thrive for centuries. Later an image of the value that regenerating this relationship could bring to surrounding regions moved Raul de Villafranca to articulate La Palmilla's vocation as *reweaving people with place.*

Draw on legacies. The cultural, spiritual, and philosophical foundations of a place can become sources of new spirit. Is there a legacy that may have faded but still has resonance for people? If it was reawakened, what would it inspire? What does this tell us about what this place has to offer? What does that contribute to a larger system?

Through an agroforesty system, the El Jobo project seeks to regenerate a culture in which humans and nature are seen as seamlessly integrated. Although the region's communities have been overrun by modernization and globalization, their cultural roots are still meaningful to many. Reweaving the sense of connection enables this community to heal a rift that has undermined the integrity of an entire region.

Identify iconic events and people. Significant events or people can also point to a place's vocation. What stories do people tell that exemplify the place when it is most truly being itself and therefore most able to make a unique contribution?

La Palmilla is famous for a tree that towers over the surrounding landscape. For centuries it was sacred to the indigenous peoples of the region, and it is still revered today. This iconic being is a profound expression of the essence of this place and an important reminder of the harmony that is possible between humans and nature.

Take inspiration from the future. In places where rapid growth and a highly mobile society have created a melange of old and new aspirations, the source of vocation may be in the future. How will this place serve the lives of future generations? What about this place's unique character will enable it to serve future generations? What contribution must the community make to enable their children and grandchildren to thrive here?

EMPLOYING VOCATION AS A SOURCE OF DIRECTION

Once a candidate vocation has emerged, testing and upgrading it provide opportunities to deepen people's understanding and connection. Following are some criteria that a vocation of place must meet if it is to exert the evolutionary pull required for regeneration.

- It is grounded in a deep, pattern-based understanding of the local web of life.
- It depicts the place's potential within its region and beyond in a way that local people experience as authentic, meaningful, and significant.
- It is *integrative and holistic* in ways that bridge cultures, classes, and generations.
- It can be translated into personal aims and principles that people find relevant in their own lives and work.
- It is capable of serving as the regenerative source of direction for a project, reminding everyone on the team of their larger purpose.

A vocation of place is a powerful instrument for inspiring people to come together around a common purpose. It helps stakeholders order and organize their efforts toward a larger purpose. And it provides both the project and the community with a basis for developing principles for holistic decision making.

ENDNOTES

1. This story of Curitiba is a summary drawn from Nicholas Mang's Leadership Case Study of Curitiba, Brazil, in his doctoral dissertation, *Towards a Regenerative Psychology of Urban Planning Leadership Case Study of Curitiba, Brazil* (San Francisco: Saybrook Graduate School and Research Center, May 2009), available at http://gradworks.umi.com/33/68/3368975.html.
2. Ibid.
3. Bill McKibben, *Hope, Human and Wild: True Stories of Living Lightly on the Earth* (Boston: Little, Brown and Co., 1995).
4. Nicholas Mang, ibid.
5. Ibid.
6. Aroldo Hayert, editor, *Memória da Curitiba* (Curitiba: Curitiba Urban Planning and Research Institute, 1992).
7. Aroldo Hayert, ibid.
8. Aroldo Hayert, ibid.
9. Cited in McKibben, 1995, p. 68.
10. Nicholas Mang, ibid.
11. Aroldo Hayert, ibid.
12. Nicholas Mang, ibid.
13. Charles Leadbeater, "The Socially Entrepreneurial City," in Alex Nicholls, editor, *Social Entrepreneurship: New Models of Sustainable Social Management* (New York: Oxford University Press, 2006) p. 236.

14. Nicholas Mang, Ibid.
15. Aldo Leopold, *A Sand County Almanac: With Other Essays on Conservation from Round River* (New York: The Random House, Inc., 1970) p. 263.
16. Lewis Carroll, *Through the Looking Glass and What Alice Found There* (Public Domain).
17. Christopher Middleton and Philip Freestone, "The Impact of Culture-led Regeneration on Regional Identity in North East England," presented at Regional Studies Association International Conference: The Dilemmas of Integration and Competition, Prague, Czech Republic, May 27–29, 2008 (accessed August 31, 2015) http://citeseerx.ist.psu.edu/viewdoc/download?rep=rep1&type=pdf&doi=10.1.1.224.5737.

CHAPTER 4

THE GUILDED AGE

Each one of us can make a difference, together we make change.[1]

Senator Barbara Mikulski

Designers experience a kind of magic when a great project hits its groove and the team starts firing off brilliant ideas. Stakeholders show up and get excited. Political leaders endorse what's happening on the ground. Social media begins to buzz.

What's not often talked about, though, is what happens *after* a project gets built or implemented. When that initial rush of energy has elapsed and the various project team members have packed up and moved on, it's up to the project's immediate stakeholders—its inhabitants, neighbors, and the larger community—to sustain not only the project's functional effectiveness but also its aspirations.

Many architects have designed high-performing buildings whose features are never truly mastered by their users. Every seasoned ecological restoration professional has had the experience of returning to a restored site years later to find it degraded again. Some healthy ecological processes may have taken root, but the human activities that led to degradation in the first place may still be going on.

CO-EVOLVING MUTUALISM

One of the characteristics of regenerative development is that its influence on place continues to unfold long after a project is "completed." A project by itself cannot supply the resources and energy needed to achieve the full potential of this ongoing regenerative effect. Rather, it must call into existence a *system* of mutually beneficial stakeholder relationships. This is where the power lies to extend the project's contribution through widening spheres of influence and time.

Thus, a fourth basic premise of regenerative development is that *projects should be vehicles for catalyzing the cooperative enterprises required to enable evolution.*

> Premise Four: Projects should be vehicles for catalyzing the cooperative enterprises required to enable evolution.

To enable evolution, humans need to relearn how to be as necessary to the expression of ecological potential as bees are to the flowers they pollinate. This necessary relationship can be described as *co-evolving mutualism*, a progressive and mutually beneficial harmonization of human and natural systems.

Bees and flowers co-evolved over millions of years. In a similar way, New World ecosystems co-evolved with human management practices over many millennia. The result was the deep soils of the North American prairies and the rainforests of the Amazon Basin. Skillful use of fire and other tools coaxed these ecosystems to the high levels of diversity and productivity that humans prefer, and at the same time benefited a host of other species.

Co-evolving mutualism is a process that cannot be predicted but can be continually planned and managed toward. For example, restoring riparian areas in urban settings can reestablish wildlife corridors, leading to interactions between city dwellers and wild animals. This requires adjustments, including respecting and learning how to behave toward unexpected creatures that show up in the neighborhood. But it also makes possible the experience of connection to nature that is missing in many urban centers (Figures 4.1 and 4.2).

FIGURE 4.1 A restored stretch of the Rio Grande in Albuquerque, the largest metropolitan area in New Mexico.

Copyright © Kronosphere Design

FIGURE 4.2 When wildlife corridors are restored, wild animals can show up unexpectedly in urban neighborhoods. This requires some adjustment but also reconnects residents with nature.

Copyright © Guy J. Sagi/Shutterstock.com

As instruments for co-evolving mutualism, regenerative projects bring together stakeholders—people and groups with a stake in growing the potential of their places. For this reason, the fourth principle of regenerative development is to *actualize stakeholder systems toward co-evolving mutualism*.

Principle Four: Actualize stakeholder systems toward co-evolving mutualism.

Stuart Kauffman, who coined the phrase *co-evolving mutualism*, has pioneered the application of complexity theory to biological processes. He notes that, "Species live in the niches afforded by other species." Water, wind, and other energies shape geology to create niches that invite life—plants, animals, microorganisms. These life forms further shape their niches, and influence geologic and hydrologic forms and flows. Humans participate in this dance, shaping and being shaped by nature to produce the places we know today. Intentionally catalyzing systems of co-evolving mutualism requires seeing people and nature as "co-creators of the enormous web of emerging complexity that is the evolving biosphere and human economics and culture."[2]

These intentional systems pattern themselves after healthy ecosystems. They strive to be self-creating, self-managing, and self-regenerating through reciprocal relationships among their parts and with their larger environment. They are modeled on ecological principles, and grow organically out of the specific character and essence of a place. Just as ecosystems create cooperative enterprises to advance whole communities, humans can translate ecosystem understanding into concrete, place-specific strategies for cooperation.

To engage flexibly and creatively with the unpredictable outcomes and requirements of co-evolving mutualism, these stakeholder systems need to grow their intelligence about place. They must deepen their understanding of where they live and discover new opportunities for growing its vitality and viability.

Sociologist Robert Putnam has observed that from this deep understanding grows a feeling of connection to place, which nurtures a web of reciprocal benefits and obligations.[3] This web, which represents a very powerful form of social capital, enables a community to detect changes in its environment, come to a shared interpretation of them, and respond in a coordinated manner. The social and economic health of a community inevitably benefits from this steadily growing capacity.

CAPE FLATS NATURE

Launched in 2002 as a radical new approach to conservation in Cape Town, South Africa, Cape Flats Nature (CFN) was dismantled just eight years later, having accomplished what it set out to do. The founders recognized from the outset that what needed to be sustained through time was the *process* they were introducing, not a *structure* called CFN. They could see that they would need to move away from the centralized, top-down pattern of traditional conservation efforts and toward a living network of community-level cooperative systems (Figure 4.3).

FIGURE 4.3 View of Cape Town, South Africa, from Table Mountain.
Copyright © Marisa Estivill/Shutterstock.com

A HISTORY OF FRAGMENTATION AND SEPARATION

South Africa's Western Cape, a UNESCO Natural World Heritage Site, has been described as more botanically diverse than the Amazon rainforest. Cape Town is the largest population center within the cape. It is also South Africa's fastest-growing city, due to an explosion of economic migrants moving into Cape Flats, an expansive, low-lying area southeast of the central business district.

This once unbroken landscape of dunes and wetlands has become a scattering of 270 fragments of biodiverse habitat, interspersed among a densely populated mosaic of townships and informal settlements. Many of these are marked by high rates of poverty, gangs, substance abuse, and violent crime. Not surprisingly, Cape Flats has the world's highest rate of plant extinction. It also presents a nightmarish challenge to traditional conservation practices.

Historically, conservation has focused on preserving prominent natural systems, protecting them from uncaring and destructive humans. In Africa, this approach has only served to reinforce patterns of colonialism, as landscapes deemed ecologically sensitive were fenced off with little consideration for local communities or displaced populations. Early Cape Town conservation efforts focused primarily on the *fynbos* (shrub-land) of Table Mountain, engaging nearby wealthy white communities while largely ignoring the communities of color found in the flats.

By the 1990s, conservationists were aware that practices based on conflict and separation would ultimately fail in Cape Flats, regardless of how many resources and regulations they brought to bear. As CFN Project Manager Tanya Layne noted, "We won't find support for conservation in the Cape Flats by fencing people out."[4]

MAINSTREAMING BIODIVERSITY

The search for an alternative led to adoption of the city's Integrated Metropolitan Environment Policy (IMEP) in 2001. It proclaimed, "There doesn't need to be a choice between environment and people." The following year, CFN was launched with the mandate to demonstrate that community needs could be addressed *through* conservation. By partnering with local communities in ways that benefited them, the city would be better able to manage biologically important sites.

Formally titled "mainstreaming biodiversity," the CFN approach shifted the focus of conservation from protection to creating "a constituency for conservation among citizens who understand themselves to be living as part of natural systems."[5] They set to work, "building the meaning and relevance of biodiversity in the everyday lives of ordinary people living around nature reserves, contributing to what was important to local people, and doing it in a way that strengthened local community structures and processes."[6]

The CFN project began with four demonstration sites, selected on the basis of their vegetation, size, and proximity to disadvantaged communities. CFN spent the first three months listening to the stories of people who were familiar with the sites. This enabled them to map the patterns in each site's neighboring social system.

The CFN team then invited local champions to help move the process forward. Young black graduates of conservation programs, preferably from the communities in which the project worked, were hired as nature conservation managers. Their jobs included both on-the-ground management and staff support to the newly forming local stakeholder partnerships.

CFN made no promises to communities. It simply offered itself as "a space for people, together, to imagine what was possible."[7] Individuals and people in local organizations contributed their own time to the partnership. Their focus was on building community, weaving together "social and environmental fabrics through engagement, not just a delivery of services to a passive citizenry."[8] Thus CFN played a strictly catalytic role, never directly managing the sites or implementing activities itself. Instead, it helped local community partners identify, plan, and attract support for site activities.

From its inception, CFN was based on partnering and capability development. The project grew out of a partnership among the city, community groups, and conservation organizations. The work began by bringing together the stakeholders who were relevant for given sites—biologists, neighbors, social service organizations, teachers, and students. The precise makeup of each group depended on local conditions. Just three years into the project, 16 community organizations were actively involved in conservation projects at the various sites.[9]

Capability building took many forms, but two learning forums were key to sustaining it as a living, evolving process. In 2003, at the request of local stakeholders, a forum was set up to enable champions from different sites to share experiences and learn together.

At the same time, the project's core team provided extensive developmental support to local conservation managers. This set a pattern of mentorship that continued into the city departments that subsequently hired them. "We paid as much attention to nurturing the development of our team as we did to nurturing community partnerships," noted Layne. "This may be the real magic: the work of the project out there in the world was nurtured through the work we did internally. We transformed our external reality through our internal practice."

Once the demonstration sites had been successfully established, CFN shifted to creating institutional collaborations that would ensure that its approach would deepen, spread, and continue to evolve. Writing three years after the project ended, Layne noted the success of this phase. "New projects that focus very explicitly on reaching biodiversity targets also include elements designed to maximize socioeconomic benefits and engage community stakeholders. At all levels of biodiversity management in the city, we now see the fingerprint of Cape Flats Nature."[10]

During its brief but effective life span, CFN showed how it is possible to include people as part of "living landscapes." This approach has continued long after project completion, sustained by active stakeholders and ongoing capability development.

GUILDS

In regenerative development, stakeholder systems are organized as *guilds*, a concept that comes from the ecological design system of permaculture. A guild is a web of exchanges among a diverse range of entities, which together create the whole that sustains them. Guilds are examples of complex reciprocity, in which exchanges are often indirect and equivalent value is hard to measure.

Guilds are examples of *complex reciprocity*, in which exchanges are often indirect and equivalent value is hard to measure.

In nature, a guild might be a small community of bacteria, fungi, plants, and animals that provide for one another, the smallest knot of relationship within the living web of an ecosystem. A guild is not a wheel with a central hub through which all exchanges pass. Instead, it is a multidirectional network. One member may benefit from two or three others and, in turn, provide benefits to three or four completely different members. These reciprocal relationships do not need to be simple. The network's diversity helps to ensure that all needs are met. In a common guild found in the American Southwest, a juniper tree shelters a young piñon pine and in return gains fertility from the droppings of the animals attracted by the piñon nuts (Figure 4.4).

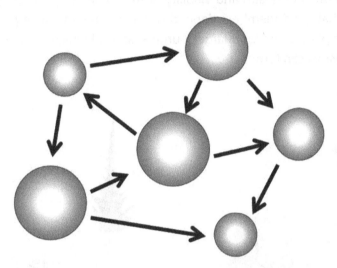

FIGURE 4.4 A guild is a web of exchanges among a diverse range of entities, which together create the world that sustains them.

Copyright © Regenesis Group, Inc.

The concept of guild applies to human systems as well. A guild of businesses, individuals, or organizations can foster reciprocal benefits among its members, supporting their capacity to invest in and be valued by the system. For example, a clothing retailer or a bookstore might benefit from contiguity and cooperation with a nearby museum, neighboring restaurants, a florist, a branch bank, professional offices, a park, and local transit. Such a strategy grows consciousness about mutuality of interest, which stimulates creativity with regard to realizing it.

In a natural guild, each species earns its welcome by contributing to the conditions that favor other members and the ongoing health and evolution of the whole. Similarly, in human systems a guild prospers to the degree that each stakeholder is aware of and invested in the continued well-being and resilience of all other stakeholders. In other words, each member sees itself as an investor in the whole.

Guilds form around organizing cores—for example a key element like an oak tree that can generate and support large numbers of reciprocal relationships (Figure 4.5). In human systems, guilds form around overarching purposes that benefit the broader health and viability of the community, place, or field of endeavor that guild members depend upon. In a regenerative project, the vocation of place provides a larger purpose around which a guild of stakeholder investors can form.

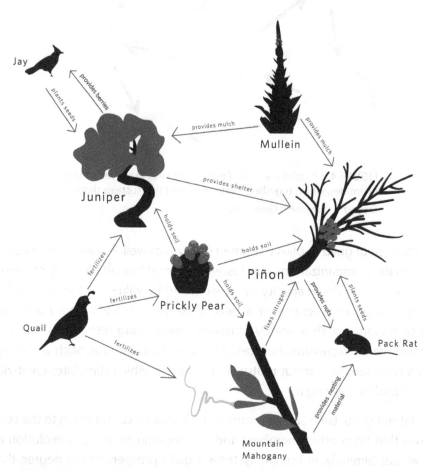

FIGURE 4.5 A natural guild in a southwestern U.S. desert ecosystem, whose key element is a species of juniper tree.

Copyright © Regenesis Group, Inc./Illustration by David Grey and Kronosphere Design

GUILDS AND REGENERATION

A coherent system of stakeholders working to grow the common wealth in a community is a powerful way to ensure that the regeneration initiated by a project will continue over time. Guilds extend the reach of a project. Through partnerships within a guild, a project is able to leverage resources and influence without added expenditures. For projects with high aspirations, this leverage is critical. Without it they will inevitably attempt to accomplish too much on their own. Participation in guilds of mutual benefit shifts this equation.

At the same time, catalyzing a stakeholder system should never be undertaken as a public relations exercise. Project developers and teams often misunderstand this key point, since they are strongly conditioned to view their relationships with communities through a transactional lens. "I'll do this for my community, and in return it will support me in getting the approvals and buy-in I need to carry out my (spectacularly wonderful, beautiful, and beneficial!) project."

Not only does this attitude undermine the goodwill that a project has carefully cultivated; it misses the real point. A project only becomes regenerative when it fosters awareness and ongoing commitment to realizing the potential within a community. With regard to that larger goal, a project is one stakeholder among many others, with an obligation to stand side by side with them as a peer. A project is regenerative when it works as a node in a network, rather than as a partner to a transaction. As a member of a guild, its contribution to the genuine wealth of its place will increase its own value.

A project is regenerative when it works as a node in a network, rather than as a partner to a transaction.

A good example is Prairie Crossing, a community of high-performance homes in Lake County, Illinois. When local building codes were proving to be more hindrance than help, the developer turned to local stakeholders for assistance. They responded, "We see your problem and the benefits of your approach. How about writing it up as a performance-based code alternative?"

The result was Section 326, the "Advanced Energy Efficient and Resource Efficient Single Family Residence Code," which gave Prairie Crossing builders the option to implement advanced building strategies, if they adopted all strategies at once. The developer benefited, and as a consequence, so did all the other members of the guild, including contractors, construction workers, vendors, homeowners, and the community at large.

FROM TRANSACTIONAL TO RELATIONAL

To activate a stakeholder system toward co-evolving mutualism requires an understanding of what a stakeholder is and what it means to have a stake. Stakeholders are usually defined as those who have some influence over a project and will be affected, positively or negatively, by its outcomes. As a result, stakeholder engagement is generally transactional in nature, depending on an exchange of perceived value. Building and community development projects usually address stakeholder concerns in one-time events, often as part of negotiations for development rights. Examples include donating a portion of the site to community purposes, granting neighbors special access to facilities, or donating percentages of transfer fees to community projects.

In regenerative development, stakeholder engagement is relational. Stakeholders are those who have a stake in *what could be*—the greater potential that a regenerative project brings to their place. They are seen as co-creators and co-investors, working together to move a project, community, and place up to a higher order of expression. Rather than engaging stakeholders separately, a regenerative project seeks to bring them together as a guild, with a shared purpose that connects them to one another and their place.

An example is the diverse stakeholder guild that has grown up around Quigley Farm and Conservation Community, a project in the Wood River Valley of Idaho. All of the members of this guild share an interest in the health of their valley and citizenry. Hikers and mountain bikers seek to maintain and improve access to the surrounding national forests and parks. Local food advocates wish to strengthen local agriculture. Environmentalists want to improve the quality of habitat, especially in streams polluted as a result of the region's history of mining. Social service providers want to ensure access to good quality and affordable housing, education, and healthcare for all community members (Figure 4.6).

The Quigley Farm design and development team sees the project as a participant in this diverse community of interest. The site concept integrates many elements that are relevant to local stakeholders—public trail systems, a health clinic, a school that emphasizes ecological literacy for students, mixed-use housing and commercial space, ecological restoration and preservation, and a working farm—and the developers see these elements as contributing to the desirability of the project to its market.

At the same time, Quigley Farm is explicitly partnering with community members to ensure that these benefits are not limited to the site, but begin to be integrated into the fabric of the community and watershed. Toward this end, revenues from the project will be used to endow a foundation whose purpose is to leverage the efforts of local nonprofit organizations and community activists for the benefit of the whole valley.

STAKEHOLDERS AS INVESTOR PARTNERS

Stakeholders provide the creativity and participation required to sustain regeneration. A project alone cannot generate a systemic change. Rather, the effort toward, investment in, and ownership of change are shared among all those who come to see the project as a natural ally, a co-investor in what they are trying to accomplish. This frees the design team to focus on what it needs to do to create a successful project, knowing that responsibility for the larger effect is now shared.

Mariposa started with the vision of an ecological village—a semi-rural neighborhood that would demonstrate ways to live sustainably in the high, dry prairies of West Texas. The original plan was to transform a badly degraded sand and gravel quarry into a live/work community centered within a common greenspace. But when the design team looked more deeply into its motivation, it became clear that the project was really about education.

The team reframed the project as a school and formed partnerships with nearby colleges and universities to create a campus for field learning. Their aim was to provide a place where students could practice the design, construction, and ongoing management of a regenerative community, educating themselves, as well as the neighboring city of Amarillo.

The project's mission to provide earth-based education has attracted a growing circle of stakeholder partners, including civic organizations, financial investors, environmental groups, and community advocates. By shifting from housing development to campus, the project has pulled together a diverse stakeholder guild. They share an interest in transforming the site and communicating what gets learned to other communities in the region.

Regenerative development reveals potential investors who would ordinarily go unrecognized. Conventional projects tend to view investment through the narrow lens of money. Recognizing the full range of stakeholders and the diversity of contributions they are capable of making transforms investment from a purely transactional process to one that integrates multiple forms of capital. This awareness provides a new perspective on the exchanges that a project engages in, and opens doors to positive, collaborative community change.

> Regenerative development reveals potential investors who would ordinarily go unrecognized.

▓ WEALTH REDEFINED

Regenerative development grows new resources and new conditions for well-being—new *wealth*. It concentrates on investment rather than conservation and seeks to create instruments for growing the "commonwealth" of a place.

When Playa Viva set out to regenerate the estuaries along its borders, it wasn't only reviving a critical element in the lifecycles of fish and other marine animals. It was also planting a powerfully effective carbon sink that will continue to perform and expand for generations to come. Such an estuary is a good example of commonwealth because it improves local fisheries, improves water quality, stabilizes the land, and protects the local community from storm surges.

More and more, cultures are tending to define wealth narrowly, in terms of financial capital. Yet most people intuitively know that wealth is based on more than money. In fact, most economists recognize that, unlike other forms of capital, financial capital has no intrinsic value. As environmental activists like to say, "when the last tree dies, the last river is poisoned, and the last fish is caught, then we'll realize that we can't eat money."[11] Regenerative development, borrowing a term from economist Mark Anielski, seeks to create "genuine wealth," which is defined as all of the conditions of well-being or quality of life that sustain vibrant, prosperous, resilient, and sustainable projects, ecologies, communities, and economies in harmony with each other.[12]

"Genuine wealth" is defined as all of the conditions of well-being or quality of life that sustain vibrant, prosperous, resilient, and sustainable projects, ecologies, communities, and economies in harmony with each other.

Mark Anielski

Genuine wealth is grown from the simultaneous development of multiple forms of capital, which work together as a dynamic system (Figure 4.6). Economic theorist Neva Goodwin has articulated her vision of this system as a set of five capitals:

- *Social capital*—the capacities to foster cooperation, trust, and mutual benefit among people and groups whose interdependent efforts are needed to achieve common goals
- *Natural capital*—the web of living systems that generate, provide sustenance for, and enable the evolution of life
- *Produced capital*—assets, such as buildings, tools, and infrastructure, that enable the flow of goods or services
- *Human capital*—the health and capacity of individuals, which can be grown through education, training, development, and experience
- *Financial capital*—money invested to provide goods and services or to produce other forms of capital return.[13]

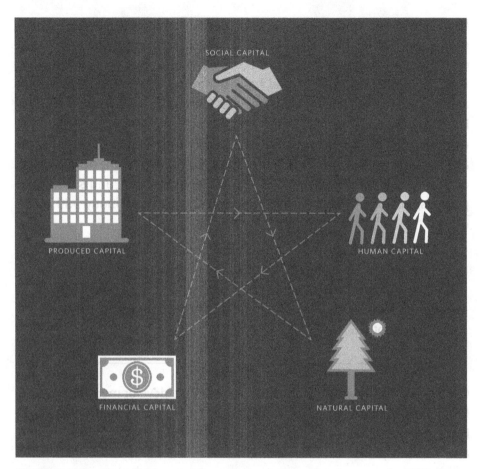

FIGURE 4.6 Genuine wealth is grown from the simultaneous development of multiple forms of capital, which work together as a dynamic system.

Copyright © Regenesis Group, Inc./Illustration by David Grey

The creation of genuine wealth depends upon the balanced development of all five forms of capital. Financial capital contributes to increasing community wealth when it is invested to grow human, social, natural, or built capital, as well as new financial capital to reinvest in these purposes.

The idea of five capitals is gaining currency among economists and now shows up in United Nations economic development initiatives. The framework makes it easier for communities to become conscious of the systemic effects of decisions and actions. This enables them to design for *solution multipliers*, leveraged actions or interventions that grow multiple forms of capital simultaneously. It also helps to avoid the pernicious habit of externalizing the negative effects of narrow financial decisions.

CREATING A GUILD AT EL JOBO

Chapter Three introduced Raul de Villafranca, a Mexico City–based architect and practitioner of regenerative development. His El Jobo project, located in La Palmilla in Veracruz, was conceived as a catalyst for initiating an ecological agro-forestry industry in order to revitalize the region's economy and provide a bulwark against recent incursions by destructive, extractive industries. The project didn't have the financial resources to make this happen on its own, so Villafranca set to work figuring out how to attract a critical mass of key players and resources. What follows is the description of a planning exercise carried out by Villafranca and Regenesis to address this critical question.

Villafranca had spent decades working in the Rio Bobos watershed to protect its archaeological and biological resources. In the process he had built a network that includes local residents and activists, academics and researchers, and policy makers at the highest levels of government. This earned him the respect and credibility needed to call together key stakeholders to form a viable guild. In order to define this nascent guild, Villafranca used the five capitals framework to identify individuals and groups with a mutual interest in establishing a heritage agro-forestry system. In particular, he looked for those that would be key to developing the kind of regional infrastructure required for the success of such a system.

He began by creating a movie in his mind of the ecological agro-forestry industry as if it already existed. Next, he described the different classes of stakeholder he thought this guild would need to include: local *campesino* groups, regional food processors and distributors, local tourism businesses, regional research institutions working on agricultural innovation, and agencies charged with managing the ecological preserve surrounding the river. To make his thinking more concrete, he then named specific people within each of the stakeholder classes who he believed could contribute to growing the appropriate industry infrastructure. As a way of seeing the role they could play as co-investors, he used the list of five capitals to identify what they had to invest and what they would be looking for in return.

For social capital he identified a couple of *campesino* leaders, along with the head of a historic society who was engaged in the preservation and enhancement of local culture. For natural capital he identified officials responsible for protecting the wild areas and river. He also had close ties to local environmental groups and spoke of a river guide who was passionate about regenerating the local culture of land stewardship. For produced capital he identified an underutilized warehouse, and processing facilities and equipment in the area. He also mentioned several local hotels that would be natural stakeholders in an eco-tourism initiative.

For human capital he mentioned a colleague at the technical university in Jalapa, who had a strong interest in training farmers in the skills needed to manage a complex agro-forestry production system. He also identified a couple of international conservation organizations with expertise in marketing ecologically produced products and eco-tourism. For financial capital he felt an established agricultural distribution company might invest in the development of high-value specialty products. The local tourism office might invest in marketing the region as an eco-tourism destination. And, of course, a key financial stakeholder would be the people willing to buy or build houses in Villafranca's project, along with consumers of the region's products.

He then tested his thinking by making a quick sketch of the probable, mutually beneficial relationships that could be established among these stakeholders. The *campesinos* would benefit from training provided by the university. The distributors would benefit from the higher-value products that the *campesinos* would then be able to grow (Figure 4.7). Conservationists had an interest in the ecological land management practices of agro-forestry. Eco-tourism companies had a stake in the work of conservationists. Hotels or warehouses would benefit from putting their facilities to better use. Purchasers of homes and businesses banked on the increased desirability of a regenerated community.

FIGURE 4.7 The *campesinos* who would be members of the El Jobo project's stakeholder guild would benefit from agricultural training provided by the university. In turn they would provide a benefit to distributors in the form of higher-value farm products.

Copyright © Raul Villafranca

Just as with a guild in nature, the returns were not always direct; instead they grew out of the development of a system involving the investment and rein-vestment of all five capitals. The exercise helped Villafranca generate a very clear and concrete picture of potential stakeholder investors. In addition, he could see that by enlarging the circle of participation in his planning process and designing an effective engagement process, he didn't have to wait to start growing a guild. He could move toward that benchmark as a part of the planning work that he had already committed to.

GUIDELINES FOR APPLYING THE PRINCIPLE

Attracting a guild of stakeholder investors is an essential component of all truly regenerative projects. It is a process with four steps.

Anchor thinking to the future. Rather than dwell in what exists today, bring into mind the larger purpose of your project. What particular future is it intended to create for its place? Envision this future in concrete images, as if it was present today and the project was up and running, carrying out its role as an integral part of its place. It is most productive to do this as a conversation, starting within but not limited to the design team.

This future serves as the initial parameter for identifying potential guild members. Without a connection to a shared end state, it is easy for a guild to become an instrument for the mutual benefit of its members, yet fail to support co-evolving mutualism with their place.

Start general, then go to specifics. With the image of a particular future as context, use the five forms of capital to map out the kinds of stakeholder that will be necessary contributors. Will you need funders? Workers? Scientists, historians, or business leaders? Once you have sketched these roles in general terms, identify specific individuals and groups that could take them on and would probably want to be involved, given what they are working on.

Test the wholeness of the map by asking if the envisioned guild will contribute to genuine wealth by helping to grow all five capitals.

Map relationships. Map the mutually beneficial relationships that could be established among these stakeholders. Starting with your own project, identify what capitals each will be able to invest and what they would be looking for in return. Map the web of relationships as it emerges to create a concrete image of the guild that you are seeking to bring into being.

Catalyze the guild. A stakeholder guild should grow the resources, energy, and creativity available to its members and the project. Look for a strategic opportunity that would catalyze a group of key stakeholders and potential champions, one that could simultaneously move the project and the guild forward by providing them with the experience of working together co-creatively.

ENDNOTES

1. Senator Barbara Mikulski, "Senator Mikulski, Afghanistan's First Lady Ruk Ghani Headline 2015 NDI Awards Luncheon," National Democratic Institute (accessed March 5, 2016), www.NDI.org/2015-MKA-Luncheon-story
2. Stuart A. Kauffman, "Beyond Reductionism: Reinventing the Sacred," Edge.com, November 12, 2006 (accessed August 31, 2015), http://edge.org/conversation/beyond-reductionism-reinventing-the-sacred.
3. Robert D. Putnam, *Better Together: Restoring the American Community* (New York: Simon & Schuster, Inc., 2003).
4. Peter Coles, "Cape Town: Garden Wonderland in the Midst of Urban Sprawl," *The New Courier*, UNESCO.org (accessed August 31, 2015), http://portal.unesco.org/en/ev.php-URL_ID=30534&URL_DO=DO_TOPIC&URL_SECTION=201.html.
5. Tanya Layne, "Ordinary Magic: The Alchemy of Biodiversity and Development in Cape Flats Nature," *Solutions Journal* 4/3, June 2013, pp. 84–92.
6. Ibid.
7. Ibid.
8. Ibid.
9. Ash Center for Democratic Governance and Innovation at Harvard Kennedy School, Government Innovators Network: A Forum for Innovation in the Public Sector (accessed August 31, 2015), www.innovations.harvard.edu/cape-flats-nature.
10. Ibid.
11. Ralph Osborne, *Who Is the Chairman of This Meeting? A Collection of Essays* (The Neewin Publishing Company, Ltd., 1972). A chapter called "Conversations with North American Indians" contained comments made by Alanis Obomsawin, who was described as "an Abenaki from the Odanak reserve, seventy odd miles northeast of Montreal." (The book uses the spelling Obomosawin.) Obomsawin employed a version of the saying while speaking with Ted Poole.
12. Anielski Management: Building Communities of Genuine Wealth (accessed August 31, 2015) www.anielski.com.
13. Neva R. Goodwin and Global Development and Environment Institute, "Capital" 2006 (accessed August 31, 2015), www.eoearth.org/article/Capital.

PART TWO

CREATING REGENERATIVE PROCESSES

Designers use their training to improve everything from shoes to subway systems. But they don't often bring this same expertise to the design process itself. Design thinking has helped reorient the process from products to users. The next step is to redefine the concept of *user* to include the networked complexity of a living world.

Designing the design process is critically important because, in a mostly unconscious way, the process sets limits to what gets created. If we are to become regenerative, how must we evolve our thinking about design? What will be necessary for coevolution?

103

*Design is not about artifacts anymore but about a process . . . (it) is not a
noun but a verb. The myth of the lonely genius is an old model.*

Manuel Großman and Martin Jordan[1]

In 2012, Metro Vancouver, the water authority for the multiple municipali-
ties that make up Vancouver, British Columbia, was on a tight schedule to
build an urgently needed sewage plant. The project, Lions Gate Secondary
Wastewater Treatment Plant, was required to meet ambitious environmental and sustainability goals, and it was almost guaranteed to attract opposition to increased utility rates from a variety of community organizations
(Figure D.1).

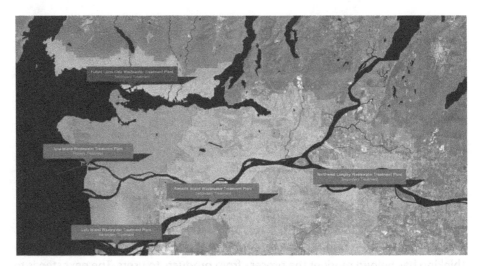

FIGURE D.1 Location in British Columbia of Metro Vancouver's Lions Gate Secondary
Wastewater Treatment Plant.
Copyright © The Miller Hull Partnership

John Boecker, a member of 7group, and Bill Reed were asked to facilitate a
process to reconcile the competing interests and agendas that could sink the
project. Boecker and Reed, sustainable design pioneers, knew that a radically
different outcome would require a radically different design process. This
project offered a rare opportunity to take a new approach.

Boecker and Reed had frequently argued that the processes we use determine what we work on and how we work. They committed to hold firm to a

process that could deliver transformative results, knowing full well that they would get pushback from both the design team and Metro Vancouver.

The project contract spelled out approximately 320 distinct deliverables, all of which had to be completed within 18 months. In the face of this pressure, Boecker and Reed made the bold decision to rein in the designers and slow down the process. Under their leadership, the team invested four months in a deep exploration of the project's real potential. Very early in the process, one of the project architects had the realization, "We're not doing sewage treatment, we're sourcing freshwater!"

With this image as an anchor, the team was able to articulate a common purpose. They explored the ecological and social dynamics that made the site unique and created shared principles that were later embedded in the design. Out of this intense effort came nine evocative "themes" that inspired the design team to develop nine entirely new approaches to municipal wastewater treatment.

Each of the themes described an approach that was simultaneously pragmatic, holistic, creatively stimulating, and compelling to local stakeholders. For example, one theme, *Ant Colony*, emphasized the potential for synthesizing ecology and industry on the site. The idea was to provide "social and technical resources that [would] . . . support an entrepreneurial and interdependent business district."[2] Another theme, *Urban Garden*, described the potential for a highly productive site that would make the nutrients in sewage available for agricultural uses "in a manner that is inspiring, educational and behavior-changing."[3] The ultimate goal was to merge all nine themes into one synergistic and unified concept.

While this preliminary work was going on, the engineers had been chomping at the bit. Treatment technologies were well known to them and they could see no reason to over think obvious solutions. But they astonished themselves. By the end of the process, they had come up with nine new engineering approaches, each responding to one of the larger themes. Although earlier they had questioned the usefulness of the process, they were now fully on board.

On the face of it, Boecker and Reed's initial decision to slow down seemed counterintuitive. But they knew that the predesign phase was critical, if the team was to break out of the box that its high-level professional experience had created. Their insistence paid off. In the end, the process yielded on-time delivery of a massive and complex project, with almost none of the anticipated change orders, and rare unanimous approval by the Metro Vancouver board.

This was possible, in part, because the client team understood that this plant needed to be more than a conventional industrial site, surrounded by a gray concrete-brick wall, crowned with concertina wire, and emitting offensive odors. They envisioned a beautiful object, a building perhaps. Eventually, the design process helped them see the plant as a node, an active and dynamic member of the community with an important role to play.

Along with the designers, the client team wrestled with how to make the plant a source of freshwater for the nearby creek and an island of green within the surrounding industrial zone. They wanted it to provide useful raw materials. Little by little, they developed the image of an attractor point, a place where people would come together to learn, interact, and build community. One of the designers joked that the sewage plant should be a place where couples would come to get married. "Why not?" responded other members of the team, "It's a worthy standard to hold ourselves to!" (Figure D.2).

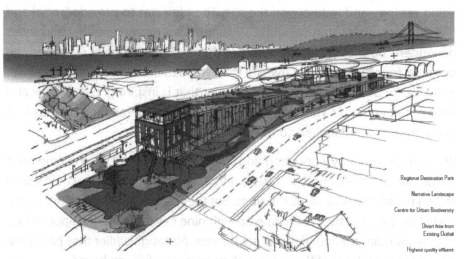

Regional Destination Park

Narrative Landscape

Centre for Urban Biodiversity

Divert flow from Existing Outfall

Highest quality effluent

FIGURE D.2 One designer joked that the Lion's Gate water treatment plant should be a place where couples would come to get married. "Why not?" responded others, and the team made it a design standard.

Copyright © The Miller Hull Partnership

Through its visionary sense of purpose, especially as portrayed through the themes, the project helped align 21 diverse but interrelated communities. It created a shared direction that allowed them to work together, while orienting them to how the plant could be much more than simply a functional way to process waste. At the same time, the project's vision was supported by sophisticated metrics that demonstrated its ability to deliver both quantitative and qualitative value.

As a result, the community engagement process generated far less conflict and controversy than would otherwise have been the case. For example, some citizen watchdog groups that had been strongly skeptical of the cost/benefit ratio, came to see the plant as a multifaceted community asset. As a result, permitting and community approvals were completed 18 months ahead of schedule.

The project purpose also created alignment among the design and client teams' diverse members, most of whom were accustomed to carrying out their tasks within their professional silos. For example, the engineers had seen this as a mechanical problem, while the architects saw it in terms of aesthetics and design. This fragmentation, which is characteristic of the development industry, was the reason why the contract had originally spelled out 320 distinct deliverables.

By organizing the planning process around a series of workshops, as well as a carefully constructed work plan, the team was able to leverage its efforts. The architects and engineers together set such high standards that they had no choice but to join forces in order to achieve them. This level of integration across disciplines ended up significantly reducing the number of deliverables (by at least 50 percent), while increasing the project's overall coherence and intelligibility.

Such a powerful process inevitably had an impact on participants, many of whom were transformed. One of the project managers, an engineer, had always measured success in terms of "getting things done." But by the fourth workshop she was holding people accountable for the quality of their conceptual thinking. She had come to see the power of moving thinking upstream in order to create better design downstream.

The board of Metro Vancouver had always worked through proxies, taking a hands-off approach to the design and execution of projects. "Show us the design and we'll let you know if we approve of it," had been the management philosophy. Boecker and Reed tried mightily to break this pattern by inviting the board to work with them in order to evolve its aims and visions for Lions Gate. They were soundly rejected, but by the time the project was completed, the board had evolved its governance and become more participatory.

One of the project's most powerful effects occurred within Metro Vancouver's Public Information Department (PID). Because large public infrastructure projects often generate controversy, PID had traditionally managed public engagement very tightly. Communities were invited to comment on designs after the fact, and information was shared on a need-to-know basis.

Boecker and Reed, on the other hand, saw public engagement as an opportunity to grow collective intelligence about the potential that this project could realize. In the first public meeting, they laid out the purpose that the team had developed for the project and the process by which they hoped to accomplish it. Community members were disarmed by this transparency, and expressed relief and excitement that they were invited into the dialogue. After the session was over, Boecker and Reed were told in no uncertain terms that they would be leading no more community meetings. They had inadvertently violated every rule for working with communities and created a situation that felt to PID abnormal and inappropriate.

However, their inadvertent error also made it difficult for PID to go back to business as usual. The community had been invited and there was no way to uninvite it. Project architects and PID stepped up and engaged in an unfolding process that included the public in a series of open meetings. Together they explored community needs and potential. This developmental approach built overwhelming public support, an effect that was not lost on PID. As a result, it changed its policies to embrace transparent public involvement in all future projects (Figure D.3).

Perhaps the most enduring changes occurred within the design team members themselves. The importance of the project had attracted professionals of international stature, including Miller Hull and space2place, who led the

This build scenario

**ENGAGES THE COMMUNITY
IN AN ACTIVE PARTNERSHIP**

so that mutually beneficial opportunities for Metro
Vancouver and the community are created and
realized by testing the potential of the project to act
as a catalyst to strengthen social connections and
build strong community partnerships.

Secondary Wastewater Treatment
- Liquid Treatment: Deep Tank Activated Sludge technology with
  Stacked Secondary Clarifiers
- Solids Treatment: Thermophilic Anaerobic Digestion technology
  utilizing biogas to produce electricity and heat
- "Big Tanks" accommodate future changes/advancements in
  treatment technologies

Integrated Resource Recovery
- Incorporates co-digestion of Source Separated Organics as
  feedstock for additional energy production
- Introduces side stream treatment for a portion of the secondary
  effluent to produce higher quality effluent
- Makes low grade effluent heat available for plant use and/or
  district heating systems

Sustainability Targets
- Provides public places that enhance the social and aesthetic
  potential for large facilities in a vibrant urban development
- Creates potential employment opportunities for the local
  community through programs and uses on the site
- Enhances the local ecology by providing nurseries that could
  provide plant materials for lower mainland restoration projects

Community Integration
- Strengthens relationships with a variety of community partners
  through programs & spaces that have mutually beneficial uses
- Connects the community with the shoreline through a viewing
  platform accessible to all
- Potentially mitigates noise & aesthetic impacts from industrial
  activity in the port on the surrounding community

FIGURE D.3 Metro Vancouver's public engagement process for the Lions Gate project built overwhelming public support, resulting in a decision to embrace transparent public involvement in all future projects.

Copyright © The Miller Hull Partnership

Architecture & Community Integration team, along with AECOM and CH2M-Hill, who led the Engineering team. These designers said later that this was the greatest project they had ever worked on. It engaged them in profoundly meaningful collaboration with one another, which gave them more strength and creativity than they could possibly have had individually. A number of them have continued to pursue a regenerative approach to development and have themselves become pioneers in the field.

Note

Building a world that is different from the one we've built so far calls for a different approach. This is why designing the design process is as important a responsibility as designing the project itself. The principles laid out in the following chapters and the stories that illustrate them are intended to spark a new way of thinking about design and provide a basis for the evolution of regenerative design processes.

ENDNOTES

1. Creative Morning Berlin #5: Manuel GroBman, Martin Jordan, December 2011 (accessed March 12, 2016) https://vimeo.com/33611054
2. Miller Hull Partnership, LLP, "Concept 4. Ant Colony: A Synthesis of Ecology and Industry" (unpublished concept board, Lion's Gate Secondary Wastewater Treatment Plant project, n.d.).
3. Miller Hull Partnership, LLP, "Concept 2. Luminous Breathing Organism: A Constantly Variable Resource (unpublished concept board, Lion's Gate Secondary Wastewater Treatment Plant project, n.d.).

CHAPTER 5

START FROM POTENTIAL

If the doors of perception were cleansed everything would appear to man as it is, infinite.[1]

William Blake

Design is often defined as creative problem solving. Problems attract energy and attention, and the more serious and widely recognized they are the easier it is to gather resources to work on them. Sustainability and environmentalism emerged from the recognition of the problems created by modern economic, industrial, and land-use practices. Focusing attention on these has yielded major technical and social advances, and it is now possible that we have the technologies required to eliminate the waste, depletion, and toxicity created by human activities.

Thus, it is not surprising that most sustainability work continues to respond to problems. Many new opportunities arise from attempts to solve a problem. For example, much of the market for energy- or water-saving technologies has grown out of the desire to reduce spending on scarce and costly resources.

There is a hidden downside to this approach, because it dictates a future based on past and present problems rather than entire ranges of possibility. Humans are wildly creative, but our solutions orientation keeps us working within a far too restrictive frame.

STARTING WELL

The philosopher Plato once noted that, "The beginning is the most important part of the work." A generally accepted assumption is that the first phase of a design project is discovery. A team explores and refines its ideas, testing to determine how the project should proceed. This phase—which can include research, due diligence, feasibility studies, site assessments, programming, and often much more—establishes most of the parameters within which the design unfolds. In this way, it frames the thinking that will follow.

For example, someone might have the idea to open a new grocery store in order to fill a gap in the local market. She will explore neighborhood demographics, pedestrian and vehicular traffic, land costs, and city ordinances. This will help her determine the feasibility of her idea and the ways she may need to adapt it.

New standards and access to "big data" have increased the sophistication of the discovery phase. Designers can do very fine-grained analyses of buying patterns, soil profiles, or housing absorption rates to test and refine their ideas. But they rarely examine the *source* of the initial idea, and although it determines everything that follows, the generative process that originates an idea is rarely analyzed or thought about.

For regenerative development, the real beginning of a project is in the nature of thinking—the DNA—that gave birth to the initial idea. Does it arise from the need to address a problem, to fix or improve what exists? In the case of a grocery store, is it bringing a proven solution to an underserved community? Or does it come from the desire for new ways to generate life and health? In other words, is it defined by existence or potential? Either can contribute to a more sustainable world, but only potential leads to regeneration.

When approaching these questions regeneratively, one sets aside the fixed idea of grocery store and looks first at the phenomena. What is the character of this neighborhood, and what prevents it from living out its potential? Does it need a grocery store or something else entirely, such as a farmers market or a robust community garden program? To be an agent of positive transformation, what kind of grocery store would it be? How would it be laid out? How big would it be? What products and services would it offer? These questions lead to a very different kind of result than do attempts to shoehorn an existing business model into a new locale.

Regenerative development is about growing the capability of living beings—humans, communities, ecosystems—to co-evolve toward ever higher orders of diversity, complexity, creativity, and life. In other words, *regeneration is the process by which potential gets moved into existence*. It's not that existing problems aren't important. It's just that starting from the potential that we see in a situation provides a completely different context for how we address those problems.

For example, highway construction near a small lake in a mountain valley above Mexico City was exacerbating an already existing water pollution problem. The state government wanted to address the problem through biological wastewater treatment, pond aeration, rain gardens for runoff, and reforestation in the upper catchment. Though these methods offered an appropriate and effective solution, a team of Mexico City–based regenerative practitioners could see far more potential in the situation.

The lake lay within an *ejido*, the traditional land base of an indigenous tribe. Through this rural place, the highway was expected to carry traffic of a million people a day. Restoration of the lake and its catchment offered travelers a rare and inspiring example of ecological design that was at the same time consistent with the traditional land stewardship values of the *ejido*. The team proposed developing the entire valley as an ethno-eco-tourism destination, creating an educational and recreational resource in close proximity to Mexico's largest population center. This would also improve the *ejido*'s economic base and bolster the tribe's culture and values. The process for cleaning up the lake remained the same, but it became nested within a larger process of realizing its true potential.

BEYOND PROBLEM SOLVING

A problem-solving orientation causes us to look backward while the world evolves forward. Systems theorist and professor of organizational change Russell Ackoff described most planning as riding "into the future facing the past. It's like trying to drive a train from its caboose."[2]

Focusing on problems may eliminate what we *don't* want, at least for a while, but there's no guarantee that it will bring about the systemic changes required to sustain the quality of life that we *do* want. Fertilizer, for example, is used to "solve" the problem of soils depleted by overuse and mono-cropping. But fertilizer often creates its own cascade of problems in natural systems, including water pollution and further depletion of soils. By shifting focus away from the need to supply nutrients to impoverished soil and onto the potential for a healthy biotic community, we open space for a radical shift. Farming could become the means for creating vibrant living systems. For example, many perennial agriculture systems are specifically designed to enable plants to do the work of improving soil fertility, while simultaneously improving habitat health, stabilizing watersheds, and sequestering carbon.

Starting with "the problem" can inhibit our ability to work systemically and holistically. Focusing on a problem is inherently reductionist. It brings a single broken fragment to the foreground and fails to account for the context or system within which the problem is a symptom. For example, environmental activists in an agricultural valley at the foot of the Grand Tetons in Montana opposed a development project proposed for former farmland, objecting that it would reduce open agricultural space. The activists saw development as a problem, and naturally enough, the developer saw the activists as a problem.

> Focusing on a problem is inherently reductionist. It brings a single broken fragment to the foreground and fails to account for the context or system within which the problem is a symptom.

Rather than react, the developer sought the deeper potential in the situation. With help from Regenesis, he discovered that the land he had chosen to develop had long ago been leveled and graded to create fields. In the process, a whole series of seasonal streams had been buried, fragmenting both the watershed and the habitat. Because the climate made farming such a marginal activity in the region, the fields had been abandoned. In other words, this "open agricultural space" that the activists were working to protect was manifesting only a fraction of its former ecological health. The developer proposed that his project would restore these streams and their riparian corridors, thereby improving habitat and hydrology, the scenic qualities of the valley, and the desirability of his project as a place to live. This was a major upgrade to his original eco-resort concept.

CREATING A MECCA OF SUSTAINABILITY

Portland, Oregon, has become a mecca for people interested in sustainability at a city scale. Rather than planning for fragments, the city has worked to evolve a complete urban ecosystem. In the process, it has improved residents' engagement with the place where they live.

It was not always this way. A city report described Portland in the 1960s as follows:

> Traditional residential neighborhoods adjacent to downtown had been torn up to make room for high rises and highways, and other housing throughout the central city was threatened with demolition (Figure 5.1). Increasingly, downtown Portland was becoming a 9 to 5, Monday through Friday place with little human activity in the evenings and on weekends. Even its role as the regional employment center was in jeopardy as businesses looked for more competitive locations.[3]

FIGURE 5.1 Downtown Portland, Oregon. In the 1960s adjacent residential neighborhoods were torn up to make room for highways and high rises.

Copyright © Jeff Gunn/flickr.com Common Commons

Additionally, the air quality was bad, exceeding federal safety standards one out of every three days. Roads and highways in and out of downtown were congested, and property owners were responding to complaints about inadequate parking by tearing down historic buildings and replacing them with parking lots. "Downtown was losing its character, its charm and its economic base."[4]

This was a common story in the 1950s and 1960s, repeated throughout the United States. Cities struggled to retain vital downtowns in the face of increased migration to suburbs, with their large shopping malls and acres of free parking. Many cities resorted to widespread demolition and reconstruction. To catalyze redevelopment, their planning commissions encouraged large projects, such as sports and shopping complexes or dining and entertainment centers. In the words of activist and critic Bill Adams, new development was "typically offset by demolition of urban fabric and removal of industrial, commercial, and lower income housing uses, replaced only by parking or vacant lots."[5] Patchworks of new construction replaced once-integrated urban wholes.

For Portland, the turning point came in 1970, when strong opposition arose to the proposed demolition of the South Stadium neighborhood in order to make room for an interstate highway and high-rise apartments. When a major retailer proposed building a 12-story parking garage on one of the most historic sites in downtown Portland, unprecedented public outcry caused a stunned city government to kill the project. Residents demanded a voice at the table in all future negotiations about the development of this area.

Shortly after, a diverse group of activists and professionals formed the Citizens Advisory Committee to generate a vision of what the downtown could be. They proposed a set of planning goals that became known as the *Downtown Plan*. This shifted attention off of the current problems—congested streets, housing needs, and inadequate parking—and onto the potential of a regenerated urban core for the city as a whole.

A range of innovative and collaborative efforts were launched. Multiple downtown landowners traded property with the city to better match locations with uses (for example, parking garages on the perimeter, commercial buildings in the center). A new transit system brought people in without adding to congestion and saved two department stores from moving to the suburbs. Old Portland was connected by tree-lined walkways to newer districts and the river, and young people and families began to move back to the district.

The *Downtown Plan* brought together citizens, businesses, and professional planners. This broad participation laid the foundation for ongoing public involvement and the development of capabilities that continue to shape the way Portland does business today. By orienting to the inherent potential of its historic center, Portland was able to pivot from the devolution and depletion that was threatening the extinction of its unique identity to a revitalized downtown. This seeded the regeneration of the entire metropolitan area, including its suburbs. Perhaps most remarkable, the plan continues to be a living document, evolving as the city evolves, and continuing to inspire new levels of innovative stewardship.

THINKING BIG ENOUGH FOR EVOLUTION

The New Oxford American Dictionary defines *problem* as "a matter or situation regarded as unwelcome or harmful, needing to be dealt with and overcome." *Potential*, on the other hand, is the "latent qualities or abilities that may be developed and lead to future success or usefulness; having or showing the capacity to become or develop into something in the future." Synonyms for the word *problem* (difficulty, trouble, worry, complication) speak to current existence, while synonyms for *potential* (possibility, prospect) are future oriented.

Designing for regeneration always starts from potential—specifically, the potential for future evolution. This is based on the premise that *potential comes from evolving the value-generating capacity of a system in order to make unique contributions to the evolution of larger systems.* Potential in the abstract is an inherent ability or capacity for growth, development, or coming into being that has not yet been manifested. In more practical terms, it is a way of conceptualizing the gap between what something *is* and what it *could be*, if it fully realized its *purpose*.

Premise Five: Potential comes from evolving the value-generating capacity of a system to make unique contributions to the evolution of larger systems.

The potential of a neighborhood park lies in its contribution to the health and well-being of the human and natural communities that it may benefit and the social bonds that it fosters. As the neighborhood evolves, a well-designed park evolves with it. This implies that a park is more than its physical elements (playgrounds, benches, trees, fountains). From a living systems perspective, it also includes the processes by which it is used, maintained, improved, and celebrated over the years.

Working from potential doesn't mean ignoring problems. Any design process needs to solve problems as it creates something new and meaningful. The question is where design thinking begins. By starting from evolutionary potential, a designer creates a new context for working on problems, which are solved as the byproduct of new creative energy. For example, a lot of people think of teenagers as a problem, and in large part our educational system is designed to manage them by discouraging or containing their typical behaviors. And yet, if we think of teenagers as highly energetic, idealistic, and adaptive people who are looking for meaningful places to belong, then we have the basis for designing a new educational system whose purpose is to access and nurture these culturally useful traits.

As a rule, solving problems severely limits the energies available for creating what we really value. When problems command our attention, we easily forget what we actually want to bring about. We lose connection with the overall purpose and meaning of our efforts, and that makes it difficult to maintain commitment. By starting from potential, we focus our attention on what we value and seek ways to evolve systems to new orders of value generation.

For this reason, the fifth fundamental principle of regenerative development is, *work from potential, not problems.*

Principle Five: Work from potential, not problems.

RAIN SAVERS

Here's a classic example of this difference in mindset. Stormwater runoff has long been labeled a problem. Cities around the world spend billions on highly engineered infrastructure to get rid of it as quickly as possible. But recently this has begun to shift. Water, after all, is essential for life, and more and more communities are shifting their orientation from stormwater problem to stormwater potential. Designers are integrating elegant technologies into their projects—everything from artful cisterns to bioswales to complex pond and wetland systems. These in turn are serving as powerful pedagogical instruments for connecting citizens to this fundamental source of life, awakening an understanding and stewardship that water restrictions and low-flow toilet campaigns rarely achieve.

For water harvesting expert Brad Lancaster, rain has never been a problem. Over the years, he has converted his once barren neighborhood of Dunbar/Spring in Tucson, Arizona, into a leafy refuge from the hot desert sun (Figures 5.2A and B). Beginning with his own property, Lancaster diverted street and sidewalk runoff into swales planted with food-bearing, native trees (Figure 5.3). The results were so impressive that his neighbors soon followed suit. As a result, the neighborhood created a new identity for itself. From a sketchy reputation as a formerly segregated and then downtrodden and crime-ridden place, it was transformed to a proud example of how to live well in the desert southwest.

FIGURE 5.2A A street in the Dunbar/Spring neighborhood of Tucson, Arizona, in 1994, before swales were dug and food-bearing trees were planted.
Copyright © Brad Lancaster. Reproduced with permission from Rainwater Harvesting for Drylands and Beyond by Brad Lancaster.

FIGURE 5.2B The same street in 2006—a representative image of transformation throughout the neighborhood.
Copyright © Brad Lancaster. Reproduced with permission from Rainwater Harvesting for Drylands and Beyond by Brad Lancaster.

FIGURE 5.3 In the Dunbar/Spring neighborhood, a newly constructed water-harvesting chicane (basin) along a bicycle boulevard is filled with rainwater after a summer storm.

Copyright © Brad Lancaster. Reproduced with permission from Rainwater Harvesting for Drylands and Beyond by Brad Lancaster.

As Lancaster recalls:

> The tree planting enabled the people of the neighborhood to come together—new and old residents, alike—around a shared and worthy purpose. What made it significant is that we emphasized water harvesting before tree planting. That set us apart. Lots of communities are planting trees, but the rainwater piece took it to another level because we weren't contributing to the extraction of groundwater. Then we began to host an annual festival that featured native foods harvested from the trees right here in the neighborhood (Figures 5.4 and 5.5). This attracted a lot of visitors and set an example for the city, which started to embrace our pioneering innovations as public policy.[6]

When the neighborhood was awarded a half-million-dollar improvement grant, residents decided to dedicate the funds to water harvesting, traffic calming, tree planting, and public art that told their story. Money for resources and labor enabled elderly people and others to participate. What had been an exciting but cutting-edge project had now become the neighborhood norm, deeply embedded into its identity.[7]

FIGURE 5.4 A mobile hammermill grinds neighborhood-grown-and-harvested mesquite pods into edible flour.

Copyright © Brad Lancaster. Reproduced with permission from Rainwater Harvesting for Drylands and Beyond by Brad Lancaster.

FIGURE 5.5 Everyone is invited to participate in the neighborhood prickly pear harvest!

Copyright © Brad Lancaster. Reproduced with permission from Rainwater Harvesting for Drylands and Beyond by Brad Lancaster.

▉ POTENTIAL IS INHERENT

One way to characterize living systems is that each is distinctive, with an essence that is the source of its uniqueness. This perspective can be applied at any scale, whether the living system is a tree or a forest, a person or a city. Regenerative potential arises from this distinctive core character.

Potential is often confused with *possibility*, which is not necessarily connected to essence. Possibility has to do with what one can make something do. For example, a design team might see the possibility to build a shopping center on a hillside without asking if that is what this particular piece of land wants to be. Or a parent might dream of his child becoming a lawyer, when in fact she is at heart a writer.

We discover inherent potential by recognizing the essence of an entity and then seeing how that essence can be uniquely value-adding within its context. For example, as young people discover their own unique qualities, they begin to look for meaningful opportunities to express them. The more they can find and invest in, the better they understand their world and the more likely they are to find the fit between what the world needs and what they have to offer. This generates excitement and will.

We discover inherent potential by recognizing the essence of an entity and then seeing how that essence can be uniquely value-adding within its context.

The story of choreographer Gillian Lynne nicely illustrates this point. In the 1930s, when Gillian was a child in London, her school warned her mother that she was a disruptive influence and probably learning disabled, if not mentally ill. Luckily, her mother took her to a remarkably insightful specialist.

After meeting with Gillian and her mother and discussing the situation at some length, the specialist said that he needed to talk to the mother in private. As the two left the room, he turned on the radio and closed the door. He then invited Gillian's mother to stand outside and observe. Within minutes, Gillian was dancing around the room. Your daughter, he informed the mother, is not sick. She is a dancer and needs to be in a dance school.

In the context of a conventional educational system, Gillian was a problem. By envisioning her in the world of dance, the specialist helped her mother recognize her potential and design a path for manifesting it. The goals for Gillian's education shifted from the usual generic ones that would have ensured failure, to ones uniquely suited to her nature. She was soon enrolled in the Royal Ballet School. Later in life she described this moment as entering a world filled with people like her who needed to move in order to think. From there she went on to become an influential dancer and choreographer.

DISTINGUISHING ESSENCE FROM TALENT

It can be easy to mistake uniqueness for talent. Talent is what an individual or entity is good at, but uniqueness determines what that talent is directed toward. For example, a gifted young mathematician had a particular ability to visualize multidimensional geometries. For some years he had placed these gifts in service to extending the field of quantum physics as a researcher. But his essence was connected to helping people understand the universe. He was most alive and purposeful when awakening students to the total awesomeness of the universe and sharing the joy of using mathematics to explore it.

Each of us has gifts, just as each of us is unique. And so, each of us is at peril of being pigeonholed, coming to lean so heavily on our strengths that we never develop the whole of ourselves in order to live out our essence and potential. Thus, this young man's skills as a researcher could easily have overshadowed his calling as a teacher. His exciting creative challenge was to reconcile his gifts and his uniqueness through finding the right role within his academic environment.

These same dynamics can be seen with regard to place. A coastal community may be gifted with extraordinary views, causing it to be pigeonholed as one more attractive tourist destination among thousands. But that may have nothing to do with its essence. Such a community must discover the unique contribution called from it by the world if it is to endure the rigors of development without losing its soul.

Qualitative differences—when they are discovered and sensitively developed—offer nearly unlimited opportunities for communities to prosper. When a community is able to draw on and enhance what makes it unique in the world, it is able to offer something distinctive that no one else can. This is the path of greatest potential. By contrast, generic offerings produce results with relatively low potential that tend to peter out over time.

For example, as Carol Sanford points out in her book *The Responsible Business*, call centers have come to represent a generic service activity. A community that builds its economy around a call center finds itself in a commodity market, competing on the basis of cost with communities from around the world. That tends to erode not only the local economy, but also the very qualities that could enable the community to distinguish itself.[8]

HUBBELL TRADING POST

The Hubbell Trading Post National Historic Site offers yet another example of the potential that can be realized by integrating a project into the emerging aspirations of its place (Figures 5.6 and 5.7). The oldest operating trading post on the Navajo Nation, Hubbell had served the small agricultural community of Ganado, Arizona, since 1878. When the Bureau of Land Management agreed to

FIGURE 5.6 The original stone building at the Hubbell Trading Post National Historic Site now houses the traditional jewelry room and grocery, a curator's office, wareroom, and storage room. A two-story stone barn is visible behind the main building.
Copyright © Ron Cogswell/flickr.com Creative Commons

reconstruct the valley's long-dysfunctional irrigation system, the National Park Service saw an opportunity to add traditional agriculture to the interpretive offerings at the site. The project aimed to restore the long-neglected 100-acre farm that had once supplied fresh produce to the Trading Post's customers.

FIGURE 5.7 Stone hogans are traditional Navajo dwellings, often homes for extended families. This modified version (windows added) was originally used as a guest house.

Copyright © Finetooth/Wikimedia.com Creative Commons

The National Park Service asked Regenesis to create a farm master plan and a business plan for the project, consistent with supporting the health of the local community. Typically, a project like this would have focused on a historical re-creation within the bounds of the site. In this case, due to Park Service budget constraints, it would be necessary to lease the farm to a local agrarian. Thus, it needed to be an economically viable business. To address this need, the Park Service had proposed a generic solution: Produce alfalfa hay and market it to local ranchers.

Conversations with community members quickly revealed a renaissance occurring in the valley, as residents sought to restore agriculture after 40 years without irrigation (Figure 5.8). There was a desire to discover economically, ecologically, and culturally appropriate agricultural practices, part of a larger movement within the Navajo Nation to improve health by reintroducing native foods. A number of initiatives had sprung up. An anti-diabetes project at the local hospital featured gardening, cooking classes, and a farmers market. Local activists promoted traditional crops. At the high school, the Future Farmers of America were reviving the threatened Churro Sheep, bred over centuries for its superior wool, meat, and ability to survive in harsh conditions.

FIGURE 5.8 Outbuildings and fenced pasture at Hubbell Trading Post.
Copyright © Dan Kunz/flickr.com Creative Commons

The Hubbell Farm plan invited these partners to manage the farm collaboratively as a community resource. Instead of only growing alfalfa, the farm would provide irrigated pastures for the FFA students' Churro sheep and healthy, native vegetables and herbs for the hospital diabetes program. The flock produced wool that commanded a good price with spinners and weavers, high-value breeding stock, and lamb for a regional foods restaurant in Winslow, Arizona (Figure 5.9). Between pastures, hedgerows were planted with traditional medicinal and dye plants. As an educational center, the farm demonstrated sustainable, culturally appropriate methods to local farmers. It was designed to support generational exchanges, as older farmers passed on their wisdom and skills to younger people.

FIGURE 5.9 Churro sheep are a foundation of the traditional Navajo herding life, essential sources of food, clothing, and furnishings.

Copyright © Chuck Coker/flickr.com Creative Commons

POTENTIAL AND SYSTEMS

The potential of a place arises from what makes it unique, but it manifests only when this uniqueness contributes new value to its region or some other larger system. The potential of a project manifests when it helps its place step up to this new value-adding role.

Originally the Hubble Farm was seen as an addition to the trading post's exhibits, but it needed to be operated and maintained in a way that created no financial drain. The Park Service saw this as a problem that they, alone, were responsible for solving. Thus, they could only envision a minimal farm operation: one farmer, one crop, one customer.

Envisioning the farm in systemic relationship with its place revealed its regenerative potential. This opened the door to a whole range of reciprocal relationships that could bring in new energy and resources. It positioned the trading post as a participant within a living system, and thus pointed to a new role that the Park Service could play in locations throughout the United States (Figure 5.10).

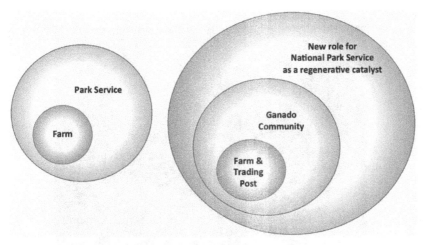

FIGURE 5.10 Nested wholes of Hubbell National Historic Site.
Copyright © Regenesis Group, Inc.

THE NESTEDNESS OF POTENTIAL

In order to make projects regenerative, it is important to think in terms of at least three levels of system: the potential of a project, the potential of place, the contribution to a larger whole. This nestedness of potential is part of the reason for the ripple effect that regenerative projects can have. Many projects fail to achieve a regenerative effect because the potential they target is too limited, focused on an element or a problem without seeing its systemic connections.

A client of Regenesis had purchased a retreat center in northern California on a splendid site in a beautiful river valley. The river, which ran through the center of the property, was threatened by development for tourism. This client wanted to protect the ecosystem, but was challenged by the need to attract a clientele in order to keep the retreat center open and viable as a business.

Rather than working on this as a marketing problem, the client worked on it by thinking in concrete images about the life of the river and the valley. The river had once supported major salmon runs. The salmon fed the valley, even as the valley enabled them to thrive (Figure 5.11). But the annual run had diminished every year and the salmon were at risk of dying out.

FIGURE 5.11 Salmon fed the valley, even as the valley enabled them to thrive.

Copyright © Lee Shoal/flickr.com Creative Commons

So she asked herself, "What contribution could my small business make to the regeneration of the river and the salmon that it once supported?" Little by little she began to envision ways that the retreat center could bring together stakeholders from up and down the valley in a unified effort to restore the river. Suddenly she was able to see her business with new eyes. As a member of a community of local river keepers, the center could help create an increasingly vital place to live and work. At the same time, it could attract, inspire, and educate guests from outside the valley.

GUIDELINES FOR APPLYING THE PRINCIPLE

The following are process suggestions to help design teams engage with the potential of their projects.

STAY ORIENTED TO POTENTIAL

A team that seeks to create regenerative projects must learn to orient to potential rather than to problems. This can require overcoming deeply engrained habits of thinking and practice, and thus it may be desirable to build agreement from the outset that this is a shared intention. Four guidelines can help a team live out this intention.

Remember what's essential. The project, the place, the key stakeholders, each of these bring something essential to the table that needs to be understood and integrated. Rather than becoming distracted by "presenting symptoms," always come back to essence. The essence of Gillian Lynne needed to be expressed in dance, but her teachers were only able to see behavioral problems. Had her mother chosen to work on those problems, the dancer might never have been discovered.

Remember the context. Keeping in mind a larger systemic context opens up a range of creative opportunities and resources for a project. At Hubbell Trading Post, a generic solution would have been to plant alfalfa. But this was an institution in deep relationship with the indigenous sheepherding culture. By seeking to nurture the well-being of the community, the resulting plan was more innovative, compelling to local stakeholders, and meaningful to national park visitors.

Value the restraints. Reframing problems as restraints allows them to become sources of creative energy. The design challenge is to discover the *value* a restraint is bringing to the mix. This often requires shifting to a larger context than the one within which the problem appears to be a problem. Brad Lancaster's neighborhood tree project was all about enabling water to do its proper work in a desert environment. By preventing rainwater from soaking into the ground, asphalt streets increased Tucson's flooding problems when it rained and its drought problems when it was dry. Lancaster turned the streets into a water collection system for his trees, and the problem became a solution.

Map the emerging pattern of relationships. Most sustainability projects start by defining measurable performance targets. However, potential is a systemic phenomenon, emerging out of new relationships among different levels of system. Moving too quickly to targets can fragment the mind's ability to hold onto those systemic relationships.

Regenerative development articulates the pattern of relationships that will replace the existing pattern when potential is realized. This pattern can be mapped in order to clarify the specific shifts in capacity, capability, and performance that will need to be developed in and among the relevant systems. Having a map helps a team maintain its orientation to potential, even as it works into successively finer levels of detail. For example, the retreat center owner who saw new potential in becoming a river-keeper was able to ground her understanding by mapping the relationships she wanted to develop with her neighbors, her staff, and her retreatants.

FIND THE RIGHT LEVEL OF POTENTIAL

One of the challenges for a regenerative development project is to pursue the right level of potential. Work on individual elements aims too low, but too ambitious a scale of change effort can cause a project to collapse before it starts. Using the nested wholes framework to graph alternative sets of systemic relationships enables a project's team and stakeholders to assess different levels of potential in order to find the "stretch" that is inspiring but not overwhelming. This taps the creativity and good will of participants. Instead of focusing on problem solving, conflict resolution, and negotiations over project details, stakeholders come to see themselves as investors in the collective potential that needs to be evolved.

HARNESS THE ENERGY OF POTENTIAL

Seeing new potential can be exhilarating and powerfully attractive, but exhilaration is temporary and can quickly dissipate. This spirit and energy need to be harnessed if they are to sustain motivation through time. Otherwise, people can become disillusioned as they watch exciting visions come to nothing. For this reason, the moment of seeing potential is a particularly important hinge point in a project. Many regenerative initiatives have died unrealized at just this juncture. The next chapter explores the critical question of how to harness the energy created by seeing potential, drawing on it as a sustaining source for a project.

ENDNOTES

1. William Blake, "A Memorable Fancy," in *The Marriage of Heaven and Hell*.
2. Russell L. Ackoff, "The Corporate Raindance," *The Wharton Magazine*, Winter 1977, (accessed August 31, 2015), www.acasa.upenn.edu/RLAscan421.pdf and www.acasa.upenn.edu/RLAscan421.pdf.
3. Office of Transportation, *Elements of Vitality: Results of the Downtown Plan*. City of Portland, n.d. (accessed August 31, 2015), www.portlandoregon.gov/transportation/article/87292 (accessed August 31, 2015).
4. Ibid.
5. Bill Adams, "7 Ways Portland Is Better than Other Cities—An Outsider's Perspective," San Diego UrbDeZine, July 27, 2013 (accessed March 12, 2016), http://sandiego.urbdezine.com/2013/07/27/7-ways-portland-is-better-than-other-cities-an-outsiders-perspective/
6. Brad Lancaster, in conversation with the authors, July 2015.
7. Brad Lancaster, *Rainwater Harvesting for Drylands and Beyond*, Volumes 1 and 2 (Tucson, Arizona: Rainsource Press, 2007 and 2013).
8. Carol Sanford, *The Responsible Business* (San Francisco: Jossey-Bass, 2011).

CHAPTER 6

VALUE-ADDING ROLES

The sustainability revolution is nothing less than a rethinking and remaking of our role in the natural world.[1]

David Orr

Seeing new potential is often described as a flash of insight, of things knitting together, suddenly making sense. Work comes alive and takes on added meaning and significance. When people connect with the potential of place, they become aware of previously unimagined possibilities. Their will is awakened and they feel a powerful urge to *do* something with what they've seen.

Ironically, this will to take action can become one of the biggest barriers to realizing regenerative potential. There is nothing wrong with will or with action—they are both necessary—but often the way we organize action by setting goals is degenerative.

FUNCTIONAL GOALS

Goals are an almost universally accepted tool for project management. Want to energize a visioning meeting? Set specific, achievable goals so that everyone knows what they are trying to accomplish. Need to convince funders or policy makers that you know what you're doing? Set goals that are measurable and time bounded. Want to assure stakeholders that you understand and are aligned with them? Set goals that are clearly relevant to their interests and concerns. Add in good systems for tracking progress, and what could go wrong? A lot, as it turns out, if your goals define project success in purely functional terms.

The generally accepted criteria for "good" goals—specific, measurable, achievable, relevant, and time bounded—can be traced back to the theories of Edwin Locke.[2] Beginning in the 1960s, Locke and his colleagues spent 25 years studying human behavior in the workplace. They sought to understand the nature of goals that led to improved task performance. Their studies were conducted primarily in industrial settings at a time when workers were not expected to care about, let alone engage with, anything beyond their immediate functions.

Locke's criteria can be useful for organizing tasks, where the effect one is trying to produce is the direct outcome of an activity. In a regenerative process, on the other hand, the value of a project is related to how it contributes to a larger system's evolution. The effects are systemic and, thus, the relationship between any given activity and an overall improvement in systemic capacity can be indirect.

Outside of a systemic context, the default mode is to set purely functional goals. Designed to be measurable and time bounded, these tend to assess value in terms of efficiency: Increase the output from this farm; reduce the energy used in that industrial process; eliminate material waste in local communities. On their own terms, these may be desirable outcomes. But they may have little or nothing to do with the improved health of a larger living system.

A project can meet or exceed every sustainable performance benchmark without contributing to the viability and vitality of surrounding communities.

For example, a new sports arena might be state of the art and net-zero, with green roofs and biological wastewater treatment, and still be at odds with its neighborhood. If it creates dynamics that are out of harmony with local patterns, such as increased traffic or off-hour activities, it may even become a source of degeneration.

Functional goals have their place in living systems and in regenerative development. They enable the completion of necessary tasks. However, regenerative goals organize work around the evolution of a system, providing the context within which functional goals make sense.

REGENERATIVE GOALS

Regenerative goals are open-ended and alive. They don't just get checked off the list when a project is completed. Setting this nature of goal requires a perspective and approach that is inherently systemic. This is where the idea of *role* comes in. A role is different than a function. An entity's function has to do with what it *does*. Its role, on the other hand, is what it needs to *be* in order to bring more life into a system. Every entity secures its place by finding a role that is distinctive and necessary for a system to thrive.

> An entity's role is what it needs to *be* in order to bring more life into a system.

For example, one can think of parenting in terms of its functions—providing food, shelter, clothing, education, protection, and discipline. This is accurate, but not particularly inspiring. By contrast, one can think of parenting as a role, "creating the conditions to enable children to develop their unique characters, well-being, and potential in order to ensure a healthy future for society." The functions of a parent may change dramatically as a child moves from toddler to teenager and beyond, but the role is continuous.

Viewed as a role, parenting requires constant interaction with a host of different players and forces in the environment. The saying, "It takes a village to raise a child," points to the system that comes into being around this activity and its connection to the future. When a father consciously lives out a parenting role, he is generating and supporting patterns of relationship that help others live out their roles—teachers, family members, other children, neighbors, the "village" that a child requires.

A focus on function is narrow and can create disadvantages in a diverse or changing environment, but a role can be expressed across many functions. For example, a worker who is skilled at a particular manufacturing task, such as operating a specific machine, is always at risk of being replaced by mechanization or new technologies. As an alternative, the same worker might adopt the role of "improver of the quality of a product." Such a role requires an understanding not only of the machines involved, but also of how operators are using them, the materials that go into the product, and the uses to which the product will be put. This is creative work. It invites a worker to develop herself holistically and builds the adaptability needed to take on new, more demanding tasks.

It is possible to think concretely about a role only when it is understood within a system, a set of interconnected elements working together toward a purpose. Each element in the system has a distinctive role to play in pursuing this purpose, which makes it both a valued and value-generating member. When the elements are playing their roles, the system gains what it needs to successfully manage the evolutionary transitions demanded by a changing world. *The continuing health of living systems depends on each member living out its distinctive role.*

Premise Six: The continuing health of living systems depends on each member living out its distinctive role.

VALUE-ADDING ROLES

Typically, designers think about projects in terms of their functions or the services they deliver. For example, a community center is a place to gather; affordable housing provides shelter to underserved populations; and a treatment plant delivers potable water. But projects can also be thought about in terms of their roles within systems. Using the same examples, a community center might play the role of intercultural connector;

affordable housing the role of safe haven; and a wastewater treatment plant the role of producer of health. Regenerative goals orient a design process toward the capabilities and qualities required by a project's envisioned *value-adding* role.

While all roles play out within a system, not all roles are value-adding. Value-adding is a concept originally developed by Charles Krone as a way to understand businesses as open systems. It names a way of working in which products, the processes used to make them, and the value-generating capability of producers are improving over time, based on customers' desires (or aspirations) to increase their own abilities. In contrast, the popular term "value added" refers to one-time events, such as converting apples to applesauce. Value-adding is ongoing and "defines life giving processes and behavior for the system and all of its members."[3]

The role of a gardener might be described in terms of coaxing the aesthetic and productive potential from the land. When a gardener purchases a shovel in order to improve her ability to play her role, she counts on a shovel manufacturer to design a product that will give her the best possible results. She might look for qualities such as balance, sharpness, a specific shape of blade, and durability. Most gardeners have little interest in the process by which their tools are manufactured. What they value is the effect that the tool delivers.

The shovel manufacturer, on the other hand, should take a very active interest in the gardener's process and how it evolves through time. This will ensure that the shovel continues to provide the desired effect in a powerful and reliable way and that the manufacturer continues to add value to the life of the gardener. Of course, to accomplish this the manufacturer will also need to engage its workers, suppliers, distributors, and other stakeholders in the value-adding quest, building their capabilities alongside its own.

For regenerative development, place is the equivalent of the gardener. As living systems, places pursue the development of their own contributions to a constantly changing world. Projects seek to play roles within the unfolding lives of places, just as shovel manufacturers seek to play roles in the unfolding lives of gardeners. The quality of a project's role is directly related to the level of systemic potential it can see and therefore pursue. The project becomes value-adding when its role is co-creative and co-evolutionary, enabling its stakeholders and its place to bring new value into the world.

Thus, starting with the predesign phase, regenerative practitioners seek to discover and illuminate the value-adding roles of all the nested systems that will be engaged in the project, including their team, the stakeholders, the project, the community, the place, and the larger wholes served by the place. As part of this process, a practitioner necessarily discovers his own role. For this reason, the sixth fundamental principle of regenerative development is *find your distinctive, value-adding role.*

Principle Six: Find your distinctive, value-adding role.

The good news is that finding a value-adding role is great for spirit and creativity. All of a sudden, a team or community group's tasks become charged with meaning because their relevance and importance is apparent. For all stakeholders, this means that will can be sustained to ensure that a project lives up to its potential.

ROLES IN NATURAL SYSTEMS

The story of the return of wolves to Yellowstone National Park provides a dramatic demonstration of the importance of one species when it is able to fulfill its value-adding role. In 1995, gray wolves were reintroduced in Yellowstone National Park after a 70-year absence.[4] Their eradication by hunters in the early 1900s had created a chain of degenerative impacts. As wolves disappeared, the elk population boomed. Unthreatened by predators, they lingered in open areas along rivers and wetlands. This led to overgrazing, loss of riverbank vegetation, erosion, and compromised aquatic habitats. As willow trees disappeared in many areas, so did beavers, deprived of food and building materials. With them went the rich habitats that their dams had created and maintained.

Within a surprisingly short time after wolves were reintroduced, this cascade of negative effects began to reverse. Hunted again by wolves, elk avoided grazing in open areas. Cottonwood, aspen, and willow forests recolonized valleys. In some areas trees quintupled in height in fewer than six years. Populations of songbirds multiplied with the increase of habitat and food. As plants and small trees grew, soil erosion slowed down. Even the physical geography and behavior of the river changed, opening niches for more life. Beavers reappeared as forests returned, and took up their role as eco-engineers, creating productive wetlands that could support growing populations of fish, snakes, turtles, frogs, and birds. Following the beavers, muskrats harvested aquatic plants for food and to clear sites for their dens, creating open water for ducks and geese[5] (Figure 6.1).

FIGURE 6.1 When wolves like these were reintroduced into Yellowstone National Park, degraded natural systems rebounded and became vibrant again.
Doug Smith/U.S. National Park Service [Public Domain]

The wolves "caused" these changes, not in a linear way and not by "cooperating" with the elk in the way that humans usually think of cooperation. By living out their role as the keystone predator within the Yellowstone ecosystem, they enabled other species to play their proper roles.[6] Being hunted by wolves shifted the ways the elk related to the landscape and vegetation, not only with regard to *where* they grazed, but also *how long* they stayed in one place. They became pruners, stimulating new growth rather than preventing it, and fertilizers of the land instead of destroyers.

A healthy landscape is able to play its role and contribute to larger systems, whereas an unhealthy landscape loses this capability. Reintroducing wolves enabled Yellowstone Park's landscapes to regain their health, and play their roles in a variety of larger systems, not only the larger ecological region, but also the national park system and the field of recreation. The impact of wolves is local, but it ripples out through nested systems.

When a living entity plays a value-adding role within a system, reciprocity is the result. It secures its own viability by contributing value. The system evolves to accommodate and incorporate it. In another example, several species of leaf-eating insects have co-evolved with California oaks. The oaks are a keystone species that provides a superabundance of protein and other nutrients to the other inhabitants of its ecosystems. The leaf-eating insects play the role of *leaf surface manager*. In periods of drought, they reduce the amount of leaf surface available for evapotranspiration and slow the growth of the oaks, which enables them to conserve water. During wet periods, the trees are able to produce foliage rapidly, staying ahead of the insects. The oaks and the insects have "evolved toward" one another, so that leaf pruning benefits both and ripples out to benefit the entire ecosystem.

REGENERATIVE CONCEPTS

A regenerative role may be expressed as a concept. In architecture, *concept* is used to describe the structural depiction of a set of physical relationships. In contrast, a regenerative concept is an idea that conveys the energy and potential of the role that a project intends to play.

Here is a simple example. An everyday item such as paper might be physically described as a thin material produced by pressing together moist fibers—typically cellulose pulp derived from wood, rags, or grasses—and drying them into flexible sheets. Described conceptually, paper is a means for recording thoughts so that they can be made permanent, reflected upon, and transmitted. Conceptualizing in this way enables one to discover and articulate a regenerative role. It shifts the orientation from things to processes, and addresses dynamics, systemic relationships, and purposes.

A regenerative project concept brings something to life for us by indicating what it generates rather than what it is made of and looks like. A concept evokes an image of what is manifesting in a particular setting. Without a concept, one can be sensitive to appearances and structures, but still not able to hold in mind a dynamic living system and the myriad patterns of relationship that make it up. A regenerative concept provides a kind of shorthand that enables a team to maintain systems consciousness across disciplines and throughout time.

A regenerative concept provides a kind of shorthand that enables a team to maintain systems consciousness across disciplines and throughout time.

Regenerative developer Anthony Sblendorio asked Regenesis to help him conceptualize a small housing project in Westchester, New York. In spite of the fact that the area was sloping terrain, it had been used for several hundred years for subsistence farming. This meant that the forests had been cleared and much of the relatively thin soils lost. When farmers were replaced by artists seeking rural getaways from New York City, the forests re-sprouted, but the soils had yet to recover. This meant that the entire system was rocky and prone to flash flooding, with little capacity to accept new development.

The project team envisioned a different state for this place, one in which everyone in the area knew how to foster the health of the forest and its soils, thus producing stronger trees and cleaner water, and eliminating erosion and flooding. The team saw a role for the project to enable suburban homeowners within the development to become good foresters and, beyond this, to teach forestry skills to other homeowners in the area. They named this *The Foresters* to describe the physical and social qualities that they wanted to build into the project and which they believed would make it attractive to buyers.

Houses were clustered, with views and access oriented to foster interaction with the forest. Runoff and sewage were biologically processed on site, and the water was used to irrigate plantings of new trees. The forest was seen as a key amenity, and the majority of the site was held in common, to be maintained by residents under the guidance of an ecological management plan. The project aimed to grow the next generation of local land stewards. Toward this end, it sited a common house at the boundary of the property, designed to host not only residents but also members of the larger community who wished to learn about ecological forestry on private land.

END-STATE THINKING

Discovering a project's regenerative potential, role, and concept requires a particular nature of systems thinking. *End-state thinking* projects the mind to some future evolution of the system that the project is working toward. It asks, "Given their unique qualities, what ends do a project and its place need to be able to pursue? What state do we need to create in order to pursue those ends?"

For example, people often intuitively engage in this nature of thinking when deciding whether to move into a neighborhood. They think about who they are (a young artist, let's say), their pattern of life (bohemian and sociable), and the pattern of life and conditions in the neighborhood (a cool artists' enclave with low rents). They think about their state of existence if they were living there (totally creative). And they think about the ends that they could pursue as a result (world fame and good parties!)—ends that they couldn't pursue where they live now (Mom's house, are you kidding?) or in other neighborhoods (gotta get out of the suburbs).

An end state is an image of what something *could* be and the ends that it could be pursuing as a result. When collaboratively developed, it becomes a pattern generator for everyone involved—team members and stakeholders alike. They become able to set their own courses, while staying in alignment with the overall goals of the larger system.

MIDDLE KYLE CANYON, NEVADA

In order to play a role that is value-adding, a project needs to be conceptualized in terms of the desired state it is trying to produce within its nested systems. Nevada's Middle Kyle Canyon, in the Spring Mountains National Recreation Area (SMNRA), offers an example. Located just 30 minutes from downtown Las Vegas, Nevada, the SMNRA encompasses more than 316,000 acres of remarkable beauty, and ecological and geological diversity, including several sites sacred to the Southern Paiute people. A few years ago, the U.S. Forest Service decided to develop a recreation-information-transportation and administrative hub in Middle Kyle Canyon on a strategic site within the forest and selected the Las Vegas–based architectural firm LGA to assist them (Figure 6.2).

FIGURE 6.2 Gateway to the Spring Mountains. Forest Service Visitor Center, Middle Kyle Canyon.

Copyright © Ken Gutmaker Architectural Photography

By the time a design team was assembled, the Forest Service had already generated 115 pages outlining the project's design guidelines and the elements that were to be part of the hub. These included an amphitheater, plaza area, interpretative displays, group picnic area, play space, educational facility, reconstructed ponds for wildlife and fishing, interpretive trails, day-use facilities, campgrounds, new trails, extensive parking, and buildings to house forest service administration and staff residences.

Using a comprehensive narrative of place to create context, Regenesis helped the design team see through this long list and associated guidelines to the real role of the project. From this the team was able to articulate a project concept that could guide its design. The Forest Service's mandate was to promote more public use while protecting the integrity of the many fragile ecosystems and sacred sites that made the Spring Mountains special. As the team began its work, it became clear that a primary value-adding role was to help visitors from the nearby urban areas make an appropriate transition to the area's natural environment (Figures 6.3 and 6.4).

FIGURE 6.3 The project mandate is to promote more public use while protecting the integrity of the many fragile ecosystems and sacred sites that make the Spring Mountains special.

Copyright © Ken Gutmaker Architectural Photography

FIGURE 6.4 A primary value-adding role is to help visitors from the nearby urban areas make an appropriate transition to the area's natural environment.

Copyright © Ken Gutmaker Architectural Photography

Rather than think of Middle Kyle Canyon as a *hub*, the team conceptualized it as a *gateway* to the Spring Mountains, offering a series of consciously designed transitions, starting from the moment visitors drove into the canyon (Figure 6.5). With each transition, they would shed a bit more of their urban perspective, gradually becoming attuned to the ecological and spiritual qualities of the place. The ultimate goal was to cultivate a sense of respect, appreciation, and stewardship within each of the park's visitors and employees, enabling them to become ambassadors for the Spring Mountains and their ecosystems.

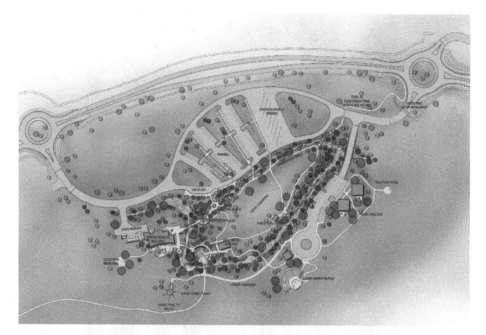

FIGURE 6.5 A site plan for the Spring Mountains Visitor Gateway illustrates the project's change in concept from "administrative hub" to "gateway," fostering gradual attunement to the area's ecological and spiritual values.

Copyright © SMVG5—Site Plan.png

Not surprisingly, given their extensive design brief, the Forest Service's representatives struggled to let go of the ideas they had started with. But over time the group was able to shift its attention from expensive "hard" features—such as buildings, parking lots, and permanent displays—to the "soft" dimensions of the user experience. This led to an explosion of ideas, all deriving from the image of gateway.

What if, instead of elaborate structures, visitors were greeted by young Paiute docents, who would introduce them to the cultural significance of the place and its plants and wildlife? What if, instead of acres of parking, a shuttle from the valley up to the mountains gave visitors a chance to slow down and get oriented? What if, instead of passive recreation, a stewardship program allowed young people and their families from around the region to learn ecological restoration and management? The more the team members explored the concept of gateway, the more possibilities they could see.

This regenerative thinking enabled the design team to develop a plan that was low impact, low cost, low maintenance, acceptable and even inspiring to tribal members, and designed to build a strong sense of connection and investment among multiple stakeholder groups.

REGENERATIVE GOALS FOR MIDDLE KYLE CANYON

In general, the goals of a regenerative project flow from the value-adding role it is called to play and the system of reciprocal roles it calls into being. Conceptualizing the role of the Middle Kyle Canyon project as gateway rather than hub elicited completely new thinking about what needed to be brought together and how. This enabled the Forest Service and the Southern Paiute people to focus the effort, setting goals that would advance only what was critical to enable the project to play its role. At the same time, it enabled the tribe, its members, and the Forest Service to discover value-adding roles for themselves.

The Forest Service came to interpret the project as a gateway for *partnering*— partnering the public with the land, partnering the forest service with the tribe, partnering communities with their government land stewards. They set a goal to co-create with the residents of Las Vegas a new relationship that would foster a strong sense of public ownership and stewardship for the health of the land. This represented a substantial shift from what currently existed, a limited understanding of the site as a place for recreation and the Forest Service as the guardian of the park's recreation value.

The Paiute participants came to interpret the project as a gateway for *regenerating heaven*, an image that had special meaning for them. Their goals included reintroducing their people, particularly youths, to the mountains as a way to regenerate the tribe. Toward this end, they also had a goal to use the project landscape as a cultural teaching instrument.

Achieving goals like these requires the participation of key stakeholders woven together into a mutually beneficial system of roles, and thus these stakeholders must be included in goal setting. One of the profound benefits of this approach is that a project doesn't have to spend a lot of time and resources convincing people of its value. The value, which they have helped to envision, is self-evident from the earliest stages. In fact, projects that are organized around a systemically regenerative role regularly garner strong, even unheard of support from local communities.

GUIDELINES FOR APPLYING THE PRINCIPLE

Design teams are skilled at thinking imagistically, conceptually, and in terms of multiple interacting relationships among elements. Regenerative development invites them to extend this practice into conceptualizing living, dynamic processes within open webs of relationship in order to express potential. This way of thinking requires subjective engagement in questions of meaning and purpose. It also requires adaptability, because it assumes that the goals of a project and the means for achieving them will emerge and evolve from an ongoing discovery process. This can be frustrating at first, especially for professionals who are accustomed to following a pre-established, "proven" method.

Following are some additional guidelines to assist a design team as it seeks to shift to a more regenerative design process.

Develop the capacity for imaging. Imaging is the ability to place ourselves mentally within someone or something else, to experience what is different from us, as it lives and works, in concrete images. It is a focused effort to sense something accurately from the inside, as it really is. Think of a great actor envisioning his role within a drama. To bring it to life, he must image his character as a living, breathing being interacting with other living beings. Imaging makes things dynamic, vivid, and energizing.

Engage "being thinking" as the context for "function thinking." Function thinking and being thinking have distinctive but complementary roles. Function thinking uses the senses to gather data for analysis, breaking things into their separate parts in order to know them. It deals with how things function and what they need to do, and then sets patterns to guide the doing. It produces knowledge, but it cannot produce understanding. For example, a beekeeper checks her hives to assess the vigor of the brood and the quantity of honey. This lets her know whether she needs to correct any problems that might be affecting the health of the hive.

Being thinking produces understanding, which requires empathy, the ability to *stand in the shoes of* another person or entity. Rather than sense things, literally, being thinking uses imaging to experience what it's like to be someone or something else, as a whole with as yet unexpressed potential. An experienced beekeeper is aware of distinct, qualitative differences in the personalities of her hives. She is able thus to discern whether there is a good fit between a specific hive and the garden it occupies and whether their relationship allows for each to better express its potential.

Once understanding is gained, function thinking allows one to lay out a course of action for the expression of potential. But without the understanding produced by being thinking, function thinking causes fragmentation, and that is always the enemy of living systems.

See everything in motion. Living systems are always moving, either evolving or devolving; sustainability is not and never can be a static state. Regeneration is an instrument of evolution. A regenerative practitioner looks to where a place has been historically in order to better understand the trajectory that it is currently on. This opens the way to discern the trajectory it could be on and the contribution a project could make to that evolution. Understanding the historical origins of the ecological degeneration of Yellowstone Park enabled its stewards to intervene in a way that put the park on an entirely new trajectory.

Don't work on the project from the level of the project. First, work to understand the living place in which a project is nested. From this it becomes possible to define the project's contribution in terms of the distinctive value-adding role that it could play. Integrated goals can then define what the project needs to deliver and how it needs to operate.

Set goals that address both existence and potential. Differentiate between goals that belong to different levels and the different natures of thinking that they require. Goals that deal with operational efficiency or with maintaining resilience in a changing environment enable improvement in the function of what is already in existence. Goals that regenerate and improve whole systems bring forth new being by manifesting inherent potential. In regenerative design, short-term, functional goals always support the goals of long-term systems evolution. At Middle Kyle Canyon, the original, entirely functional project goals filled a document 115 pages long. By discovering the potential for partnering based on the gateway concept, the Forest Service was able to discern a much shorter list of essential functional goals and dispose of the rest.

ENDNOTES

1. David W. Orr, Foreword to Andres Edwards, *The Sustainability Revolution: Portrait of a Paradigm Shift* (Gabriola Island, BC: New Society Publishers, 2015).
2. Edwin A. Locke and Gary P. Latham. "New Directions in Goal-Setting Theory," *Current Directions in Psychological Science,* 15 (5): 265–268.
3. Charles Krone, "Open Systems Redesign," in *Theory and Method in Organization Development: An Evolutionary Process*, John D. Adams, editor (Arlington, VA: NTL Institute for Applied Behavioral Science, 1974)
4. Michael K. Phillips and Douglas W. Smith, "Yellowstone Wolf Project: Biennial Report 1995 and 1996," National Park Service, Yellowstone Center for Resources, Yellowstone National Park, Wyoming, YCR-NR-97-4 (accessed August 31, 2015), www.nps.gov/yell/learn/nature/upload/wolfrep95-96.pdf.
5. Joel Berger, "Wolves, Landscapes, and the Ecological Recovery of Yellowstone," *Wild Earth* Spring 2002, Vol. 12, No. 1, pages 32–37; Amaroq E. Weiss, Timm Kroeger, J. Christopher Haney, and Nina Fascione, Social and Ecological Benefits of Restored Wolf Populations, Predator-Prey Workshop, 72nd North American Wildlife and Natural Resources Conference, March 20–24, 2007, Portland, Oregon.
6. George Monbiot, "How Wolves Change Rivers," video produced by Chris Agnos, Sustainable Human, (accessed August 31, 2015), http://sustainablehuman.com/how-wolves-change-rivers/.

CHAPTER 7

TRANSFORMATIONAL LEVERAGE

Almost always, it is a spark that sets off a current that begins to spread.
This is what I call good acupuncture . . . true urban acupuncture.[1]

Jaime Lerner

"Everything is connected to everything," declared ecologist and activist Barry Commoner, introducing what has become an environmental mantra.[2] Commoner, dubbed the "Paul Revere of ecology" by *Time Magazine* in 1970, helped move ecological science out of academic classrooms and into the world as an influential political and social force.[3] His formulation popularized the idea that human actions can have enormous impacts that we may not be aware of.

It can be both empowering and terrifying to realize that everything we do has a systemic impact. This interconnectedness is one of the reasons for the *law of unintended consequences*, which states basically that our actions always have effects that we didn't anticipate or intend. Multiply these effects by the billions of people who share our planet, and the unintended consequences become global.

The environmental and sustainability movements have urged people to hunker down and reduce their impacts. Their well-publicized imperatives, most of them very good ideas, have deeply influenced policy in countries around the world: reduce or eliminate waste and pollution; recycle or upcycle products that have outlived their usefulness; densify cities to reduce their ecological footprints; encourage mass transit and pedestrian use; and improve gas mileage in cars. Altogether, they are a creative response to the call to *reduce* human impacts.

Meanwhile, regenerative development asks the opposite question: How do we *increase* human impacts, but in ways that are consciously beneficial? In other words, how can humans serve as sources of healing and regeneration for every living system they affect?

Regenerative development asks the question: How do we *increase* human impacts in ways that are consciously beneficial?

THE REPLICABILITY FALLACY

More than two millennia ago, Archimedes famously said, "Give me a lever and a place to stand and I will move the earth." An echo of this evocative image can be heard in the modern question: "How do we leverage our efforts to get greater return from them?" Over the last three centuries the idea of leverage has fueled a stunningly rapid development of tools and technologies. It has largely been pursued through the practice of *replicability*—find a good solution and reproduce it over and over again.

Too often, the gains from this approach have come at great cost to Earth and its inhabitants. We may be able to mass-produce everything from mouse traps to skyscrapers, but the effect has been a steady erosion of biological and cultural diversity. Mass production has transformed raw materials, products, and even communities into commodities. Although standards of living have risen in the process, many people are beginning to ask whether the resulting ecological and spiritual losses are a fair exchange.

With costs threatening to outrun benefits, communities are now urgently faced with the same question: How can we leverage the impact of sustainability efforts beyond the incremental, yet insufficient, improvements that have been made to date? Unfortunately the response has followed the pattern laid down by industrialism—find good solutions and scale them up through replication.

Replicability made sense in a mechanical age, when progress and better living were thought to depend upon making "machines" work better, and machines included everything from the human body to cities to forests and farms. To do this well, we trained ourselves to focus on basic building blocks or parts. Even in ecological restoration and green building, for example, we looked at the key components of successful projects, analyzed how they were arranged, and then replicated them elsewhere.

But when projects are replicated outside of the contexts in which they arise, they tend to be resource intensive in their creation and resource consumptive in their operation. Built on imported models, they fail to reflect the cultural, economic, and ecological systems of place. Most important, by imposing pre-determined solutions, they fail to tap the creative potential of local people to design, build, and manage them (Figure 7.1).

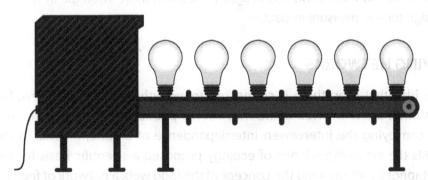

FIGURE 7.1 Replication made sense in a mechanical age, but it fails to reflect the cultural, economic, and ecological systems of place.

Copyright © Regenesis Group, Inc. Illustration by David Grey and Kronosphere Design

LEVERAGING BENEFICIAL IMPACTS

As our understanding and appreciation of the living world grows, it is over-turning the ways we are used to thinking about change and doing good. The efficacy of regenerative work comes from making small but powerful interventions whose beneficial influence ripples across systems and up and down scales. Framed as a premise, one might say, *small conscious and conscientious interventions in the right place can create beneficial, system-wide effects.*

Premise Seven: Small conscious and conscientious interventions in the right place can create beneficial, system-wide effects.

The reintroduction of wolves into Yellowstone National Park created a profound systemic response entirely out of proportion to the investment in the intervention. In the same way, the introduction of the right intervention in an urban system can create social and economic transformation. To borrow a phrase from Jaime Lerner, what's needed is *urban acupuncture*—and, for that matter, rural, regional, watershed, and national acupunctures.

So where does one begin? The answer lies in understanding not only *that* everything is connected to everything, but *how.* This requires apprehending the patterns by which things are connected in reciprocal, value-adding relationships, and then using this insight to become more strategic in how we design for and measure impact.

LIVING NETWORKS

The idea that everything is connected to everything else is not new. For centuries, the term "web of life" has been a poetic and mystical metaphor for conveying the interwoven interdependence of all phenomena. In the 1920s the emerging science of ecology proposed a scientific basis for the metaphor by introducing the concept of the food web, a network of feeding relationships by which life organized itself into ecological communities. Initially used to describe a relatively simple web of relationships among creatures that fed on or were food for each other, the web metaphor has been extended. Now systems thinkers across multiple disciplines use it to encompass all of the networks of interdependence by which species create habitat for one another. This interdependence enables them to maintain, repair, and evolve themselves. Fritjof Capra describes these networks as the "unifying set of patterns of organization that goes through all life, at all levels and in all its manifestations."[4] He concludes, "Wherever we see life, we see networks."[5]

The networks that Capra describes are, in a sense, metabolic patterns. They organize the flows and exchanges of energy, material, and information that enable life. For example, a river supports the gallery forest that grows in its floodplain by providing water, sediments, nutrients, and beneficial disturbance. In turn, a forest provides stabilization, shade, and groundwater pumping to prevent concentration of mineral salts at the soil surface. The forest's vegetation creates shelter and habitat for numerous animal species, which pollinate, cultivate, fertilize, and restructure both forest and river. The sun provides energy for photosynthesis and evapotranspiration, as well as the larger climatic cycles that replenish the river's water. These and many other elements are woven together through their patterns of exchange (Figure 7.2). The significance of pattern, whether in a landscape, organization, or body, is that it can provide designers with a framework for understanding what is sourcing life in a particular place.

FIGURE 7.2 In a gallery forest, as in all natural systems, a set of unifying patterns organize the continuing flow and transformative exchanges of energy, material, and information that enable life to be self-generating.

Copyright © U.S. Bureau of Land Management/flickr.com Creative Commons

Living networks are metabolic patterns that organize flows and exchanges of energy, material, and information.

FLOWS AND NODES

In the 1970s, under UNESCO sponsorship, the "Man and the Biosphere Program" launched an international effort to investigate cities as organisms "with quantifiable flows of energy, materials and information."[6] More than 100 studies, supporting the work of what became known as the urban metabolism school, provided quantitative evidence of the extent to which cities, and the built environment generally, were disrupting natural flows. This evidence underscored the need to reintegrate natural processes with urban activities. In a later development, urban ecology approached cities as ecosystems rather than organisms. Like urban metabolism, it focused on the growing imbalance between cities and the larger systems from which they draw resource inputs (such as fuel and food) and into which they deliver waste outputs (such as air pollution and refuse). It identified this imbalance as the primary source of environmental degradation caused by the built environment and offered strategies for more efficient resource use as the solution.

Today, growing interest in net positive design is stimulating exploration into how cities can simply reduce these inputs and outputs. This raises the question of how the built environment can "engage in . . . resource flows such that when resources are returned [to the system from which they were drawn], they support the maintenance of ecosystem functions to enable them to provide necessary services."[7] For example, instead of sending sludge from sewage treatment centers to landfills, it can be used to fertilize tree plantings.

Flows, however, are only one aspect of how a network organizes itself. Flows, after all, are only movement. *Nodes* also play an important role. They are the points in a network where flows of energy, material, and information intersect, the locations where exchanges are carried out and transformations occur. The hazard of focusing narrowly on flows, without regard to nodes, is that we come to think of networks as little more than plumbing and imagine ourselves as plumbers keeping them in good working order. For designers, nodes create opportunities to work across media, flows, and systems and to manage the interfaces *between* systems. This is where leveraged interventions become possible.

For designers, nodes create opportunities to work across media, flows, and systems and to manage the interfaces *between* systems. This is where leveraged interventions become possible.

A beaver dam creates a node, a convergence point, where the habitats for beavers, other small mammals, birds, amphibians, fish, bugs, and plants overlap. This increases the quantity, quality, and diversity of exchanges that are possible. In addition, the dam moderates seasonal water flows, traps sediment, improves water quality, and replenishes groundwater. For this reason, reintroducing beavers is a highly leveraged and cost-effect way (given the beaver's fabled industriousness) to improve both hydrology and habitat.

In an urban example, farmers markets have long created nodes. They bring together farmers, citizens, artisans, musicians, and chefs to exchange produce, plants, and artisanal products for economic and social benefit. They can be formal or casual, spontaneous or highly managed, but they are always intended to foster a productive interaction among distinct natures of flow. Farmers markets, wrote former Missoula mayor Daniel Kemmis, play a "gathering role," one that "enables people to come away from the market more whole than when they arrived."[8] When skillfully sited and managed, farmers markets can revitalize entire neighborhoods and industries, often through the ripples of increased exchange that occur as a byproduct of their presence.

Looking at the dynamics among nodes and flows reveals a system at work. This offers clues about the best places and ways to intervene in order to produce the greatest systemic leverage. For this reason, the seventh principle of regenerative development is, *leverage systemic regeneration by making nodal interventions.*

Principle Seven: Leverage systemic regeneration by making nodal interventions.

■ RECOGNIZING NODES

Natural systems are full of already formed nodes, ripe for our observation and appreciation. Some are geological in nature, others biological. A key to recognizing nodes is shifting from seeing a landscape (whether natural or social) as a collection of objects to an interrelated set of dynamic processes.

EDGES ARE NODES

Often, these nodes occur at the edges between two systems—geological, hydrological, ecological, or cultural (Figures 7.3A through 7.3D). The place in the broad landscape where the slopes of mountains or foothills meet the relatively flat plains is an example of what is called the "keyline." At this point, fast-moving water from the mountains slows down and deposits detritus that accumulates in the flatlands. As they build up over time, deposited soils are capable of absorbing more and more water. As water flows onto and is absorbed into these deposited soils, its chemistry, temperature, and underlying hydrology may all change. In other words, a change in steepness creates a node where flows slow and gather, offering an occasion for a host of new exchanges to occur.

The possibilities for exchange at a geological node such as a keyline can be greatly elaborated by biotic communities. The edges between mountain and plains ecosystems (or among terrestrial and marine ecosystems) are generally bountiful. Humans, who tend to be attracted to edges, have often colonized these zones because they recognized their inherent capacity for supporting exchange. Here they could utilize the upland forests, cultivate the lowland soils, and harness the energy of fast-moving water for milling and other purposes.

At their best, humans have elaborated these edges to improve the quality of exchange between systems. For example, early indigenous settlers around the Chesapeake Bay lit cool fires to burn away underbrush in the upland forests. This improved habitat for game animals and conditions for highly productive trees like oak and chestnut. It also subtly improved the quality of water by reducing its acidity as it moved through the carbon-rich soils. More alkaline water helped foster development of the oyster reefs that once surrounded the bay, making it one of the richest estuarine ecosystems in the world. By seeing the edge between land and sea, freshwater and saltwater, as a node, modern residents of the Chesapeake Bay could also discover ways to foster the conditions for an explosion of life in its waters and watersheds.

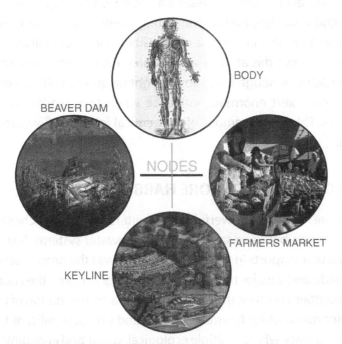

FIGURE 7.3 A through D Some "edges" that as nodes include the permeable surfaces of human bodies, market places, geological keylines, and beaver dams.

Copyright © Regenesis Group, Inc. Composited by Kronosphere Design.

LIVING ORGANISMS ARE NODES

English and many other modern languages have embedded in them a bias that causes us to conceive of living organisms as things, rather than as processes. Yet an organism is a nexus of the multiple flows that continuously move through it. For example, like other mammals, humans need material flows like oxygen, water, food, light, and heat to sustain us. We also require flows of other kinds, such as companionship, livelihood, and a sense of meaning. Each of us is, in a sense, a knot where these flows come together and are temporarily organized into a form that we call "self." These flows then pass back into the larger surround in the form of outbreath, body heat, sloughed off skin cells, affection, communication, and generative energy.

For this reason, every living organism is a node in some larger system. It brings together and organizes exchanges among multiple flows and exerts some influence on its environment as a result. Guilds, or functional associations of species, accomplish this at even larger scales. Even a single-celled organism is a knot in flows, although these flows might be quite small. However, simple organisms can exert enormous influence when they work in concert with one another. Think, for example, of how critical intestinal flora are to human digestion.

TRANSFORMING BALTIMORE HARBOR

The Baltimore Harbor is a powerful node, sheltered within the Chesapeake Bay at an intersection between saltwater and freshwater systems. Still one of the most important seaports in the United States, it was the historic center for the tobacco trade and a major transit point for immigrants into the country. Since the mid-twentieth century, the harbor has seen a concentration of investment and development, which has made it Maryland's most significant tourist destination. It is a place where multiple ecological, social, and economic resources naturally concentrate and enable exchange. But it has been severely impacted by urban development, suffering from pollution, loss of wetlands, and the collapse of native fisheries.

The Waterfront Partnership of Baltimore invited ecological design specialists Biohabitats to develop a sustainability plan for the harbor waterfront park. The brief was to introduce green technologies, such as LED lighting and recycled park benches. However, Biohabitats saw far greater potential in the situation and came back with a proposal built around sustaining the life of the Chesapeake Bay itself. "What if," they asked, "the metric by which we measure success is a swimmable and fishable harbor?" This image became the organizing theme for a Healthy Harbor Initiative, intended to create an engaging waterfront landscape. Its purpose was to educate visitors about the ecological problems affecting the bay and thus the cultural and economic prosperity that it had historically provided.

The Biohabitats team launched the process with a wildly creative project that was at once functional, artful, and conceptually amusing. It addressed the constant presence of trash that was a continual source of embarrassment and an impediment to the city's efforts to attract visitors. The Waterfront Partnership purchased an innovative water wheel system that captured floatable trash from the Jones Falls River at the mouth of the harbor. Plastic bottles, washed from streets into storm drains, were intercepted by the wheel. Biohabitats then teamed up with Living Classrooms to translate these materials into opportunities for participatory education. City youth were taught how to bundle plastic bottles into floating platforms, on which they built living wetlands (Figures 7.4 and 7.5).

FIGURE 7.4 Students planting wetlands seedlings in floating platforms constructed in part from plastic bottles retrieved from Baltimore's storm drains.

Copyright © Biohabitats

FIGURE 7.5 Students prepare to float platforms, Earth Day 2012.
Copyright © Biohabitats

These floating wetlands became nodes within the bay, enabling a number of important exchanges. There were only a few intact natural wetlands along the harbor's urban shorelines, and thus the floating islands met a critical ecological need. They transformed nutrient pollution into biomass, and at the same time, their roots supported a habitat for microorganisms that fed on pollution. Crabs, mussels, eels, and other aquatic life colonized the root systems, and fish used them for refuge. Waterfowl took advantage of the reappearance of food and shelter. Even better, these hard-working, multitasking, manmade ecosystems ran on nothing but sunlight (Figures 7.6 and 7.7).

FIGURE 7.6 Platforms soon become nodes in a thriving wetlands system.
Copyright © Biohabitats

FIGURE 7.7 Crabs, mussels, eels, and other aquatic life colonize the floating wetlands' root systems; waterfowl take advantage of the reappearance of food and shelter.

Copyright © Biohabitats

The project made an intervention to reverse biological degradation in a new, appealing, and entertaining way. In partnership with several local institutions, including the National Aquarium, Baltimore's floating wetlands quickly became a well-publicized, major art installation and an important educational resource for the city.

Biohabitats also developed a concept to transform a dilapidated wharf into a living pier to clean polluted water, provide wildlife habitat, and attract visitors. Designed, tested, and now awaiting funding, the upper level of the pier will become a constructed tidal wetland. Harbor water will be pumped to the wetland, where microbial organisms will transform and filter pollutants. Waterfalls, powered by solar pumps, will cascade over the perimeter of the pier, adding oxygen to improve the water quality for aquatic life. The entire operation will be powered by solar and wind energy.

The pier will serve not only as a node where biological systems can interact with the tidal flows of the bay. It will also become a node for human exchanges in the form of a thoughtfully designed public gathering place, educational opportunities, and inspiring technologies patterned on the intelligence of nature.

Biohabitats founder Keith Bowers later observed that the research for this project led his team into unexpected territory. For example, his company's analysis of the relationship between water quality issues and poverty was a major eye opener. Low-income, mostly black communities were unintentionally but consistently overlooked when it came to investments in ecological restoration. This was despite the fact that the areas where they lived suffered from the most severe water problems. Bowers was confirmed in his belief that environmental and social issues are best addressed simultaneously. Truly regenerative, ecological projects, when designed with this intention in mind, can help restore social systems as well as natural systems. From the outset, the floating islands project was designed to enable low-income kids to play a key and celebrated role in the ecological renewal of the harbor and, at the same time, to benefit from the educational opportunity.

NODAL INTERVENTIONS

The work that takes place at a node, the exchanges that it supports, can either generate or deplete the life-giving capacity of a landscape or neighborhood. In other words, nodes are often the best places to intervene in order to create systemic change.

The strategy of nodal interventions was core to Jaime Lerner's success in transforming Curitiba, Brazil. He wrote:

> I believe that some medicinal "magic" can and should be applied to cities, as many are sick and some nearly terminal. . . . [T]he notion of restoring the vital signs of an ailing spot with a simple healing touch has everything to do with revitalizing not only that specific place but also the entire area that surrounds it. . . . Intervention is all about revitalization, an indispensable way of making an organism function and change.[9]

The goal of nodal interventions is to create ripple effects. For example, the Curitiba design team's first and most famous intervention was the creation of a pedestrian mall in the downtown district, one of the city's most important nodes. When they closed off the streets and made minor structural changes, people returned to the center of the city and immediately adopted the new gathering place. This relatively small, inexpensive change revitalized social, economic, and cultural interactions. At the same time, it generated the energy and stakeholder involvement that would allow the team to take on much larger challenges.[10]

LEVERAGING GRASSROOTS MOVEMENTS

Urban acupuncture, as Lerner refers to this art, has taken off and become a movement. "Pinpricks of change" that flash out through a neighborhood and beyond is a strongly appealing idea.[11] It has become an increasingly popular metaphor for planners and designers looking for alternatives to costly, top-down projects that characterize much of urban renewal.

At the same time, tactical urbanism has pioneered local and hyperlocal interventions, such as guerrilla gardening, environmental art, and pop-up community spaces. Thus it is becoming more and more focused on design interventions that are spontaneous, democratic, creative, and grassroots. Depave, which started in Portland, Oregon, is a great example of this kind of ground-up effort to improve life in cities. The group removes asphalt and concrete in abandoned lots and converts them into gardens. Like the Green Guerrilla movement in Manhattan in the early 1980s, today's "depavers" are improving the quality of habitat where they live.

However, as tactical urbanism becomes more popular, what gets overlooked is the emphasis of urban acupuncture on the strategic revitalization of larger systems. As inspiring and life-enhancing as many of these grassroots projects are, their primary aim is usually to improve life in their immediate areas rather than to transform a system. For this reason, from the perspective of nodal intervention, they are singular events with limited overall influence.

The seemingly "simple healing touches" of a trained acupuncturist are effective because they draw on a complex, highly sophisticated medical protocol for understanding, diagnosing, and treating the body as an energy system. In a similar way, it is important that grassroots interventions reconnect to a theoretical base. This will allow the creative energy expended to be leveraged in order to realize the greatest community and ecological benefits.

■ SYSTEMIC LEVERAGE

Designers who understand the patterns of dynamic interplay among nodes and flows are able to transform smaller systems in ways that benefit much larger ones. They have shifted from seeing nodes as things to seeing them as knots in flows—systems of energy exchange and transformation. A beaver dam or farmers market is a structured whole, but its structure is far less important than the processes it enables.

Designers who understand the patterns of dynamic interplay among nodes and flows are able to transform smaller systems in ways that benefit much larger ones.

In the same way, buildings appear to be stable and static, but they too are knots, where flows of energy, people, materials, and ideas come together. Making a building is the intervention in a web of interconnected dynamic processes that ties this knot. This intervention can disconnect these systems from their context or it can allow them to more fully manifest their potential than they would otherwise.

For example, a primary school building that harvests rain from its roof, generates energy from solar panels, grows its own lunches, and composts its waste, is not only integrated within these energy flows; it also can help teachers, students, staff, and parents integrate with them. Seeing the context of a project as an energy system rather than as a collection of things (slopes, drainages, roads, buildings, families, school district) shifts the emphasis from a building as product to the role a building plays in enabling sustainable patterns of living.

The shift from seeing discrete things to seeing an energy system is challenging in an object-oriented culture. Yet it is crucial if we are to develop the pattern understanding of how energy flows shape places. This understanding is the basis for developing mental maps of the points in a system where even a single building can become the opportunity for significant leverage.

SEQUENCING CHANGE

Because interventions of this sort are intended to produce changes in state within systems, they must be conceptualized as more than simple actions. Designers must learn to imagine a sequence of transformations rather than a sequence of activities. Once a node has been discovered, there is an opportunity to develop a strategy, an action that will launch this sequence of transformation.

A simple example of this is the difference between how engineers and permaculture designers think about and employ gabions. Gabions are used in civil engineering as a relatively inexpensive way to stabilize soil and prevent erosion. They are essentially leaky dams, wire baskets filled with stone. Permaculture designers have long used them to heal eroded landscapes and, ideally, reverse desertification. They initiate a sequence of changes in the degraded state of a drylands system.

When gabions are placed in an arroyo or eroded channel, they cause floodwaters to back up and deposit organic material and sediment in the stream bed, where they act as a giant sponge. As the sponge becomes saturated, it allows water to gradually seep into the surrounding landscape rather than run off or be evaporated by hot sun. In the best cases, soil builds up behind gabions and erases the scars left by erosion, while the concentration of water helps to reestablish native grasses, shrubs, and trees. Once the plant communities have rebounded, wildlife also returns. A civil engineering intervention is a single action that resolves a local problem. As a permaculture nodal intervention, gabions initiate a series of transformations that can heal and regenerate an entire landscape. The physical instrument is the same. The difference is the mind of the designer.

RIO SABINAL

The state of Chiapas invited a planning group from Mexico City to help redevelop several miles of the Rio Sabinal, which runs through the heart of the city of Tuxtla Gutiérrez (Figure 7.8). The project focused on an urban reach of the river and was originally intended to address flooding and water quality concerns. It also included the creation of a park system and pedestrian corridor in the city center (Figure 7.9).

FIGURE 7.8 Tuxtla Gutiérrez in the Rio Sabinal watershed of Mexico.
Copyright © Rio Sabinal 2 Copy jpg

FIGURE 7.9 A stretch of the Rio Sabinal showing bank erosion and stabilization.
Copyright © Rio Sabinal 4.jpg

With the project team, Regenesis explored the longstanding historical, cultural, and spiritual significance of the river. This led to conceptualizing the project as a *collar de flores*, a reference to flower necklaces used by the local indigenous people in celebratory and sacred ceremonies. The flowers would be parks, strung along the necklace of the river (Figure 7.10). Each would be a node unto itself, dedicated to a sacred flower, and each would be associated with a *poza*, a confluence of the river with a smaller tributary stream that creates a natural swimming hole. In living memory, people gathered and played at the *pozas*, but in recent decades they had been abandoned because of urbanization, flooding, and pollution. In other words, the parks would regenerate existing nodes.

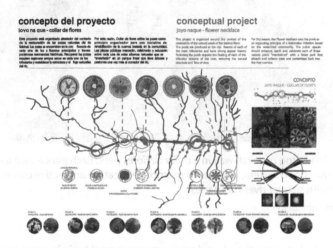

FIGURE 7.10 *Collar de flores*, a concept for the Rio Sabinal restoration project: Parks are strung along the river like a "necklace of flowers," each a node in the larger riverine system, and each featuring a different sacred flower.
Copyright © SOP—Rio Sabinal

Regenesis helped the project team realize that questions of flooding and water quality could be addressed by interventions organized around the nodes. They extended their concept for the parks, envisioning them as neighborhood centers that would promote education and active community engagement with each of the smaller tributaries. As neighborhoods restored integrity to the fabric of the watershed within their own sub-watersheds, the flooding hazards in the main trunk of the river would diminish (Figure 7.11).

FIGURE 7.11 Rendering of a walkway in a *collar de flores* park. Each park is also a node within a neighborhood system, a center to promote education and active community engagement with smaller river tributaries.

Copyright © Rio Sabinal.jpg

The parks were also conceived as demonstration and training centers for economic activities, such as food production, that were directly connected to the health of the river. In this way, river restoration was based on both community identity and culture, and the potential for new livelihoods for many of the city's impoverished citizens.

GUIDELINES FOR APPLYING THE PRINCIPLE

All designers work with nodes and flows, whether or not they use this terminology. A building is a node where flows of people, energy, water, food, information, and a host of other phenomena intersect and interact to generate new phenomena. The task of an architect is to facilitate and harmonize these interactions in ways that enable the best possible expression of life's meaning and purpose for inhabitants. Regenerative development invites designers to extend their vision to the ways that projects such as buildings can be used to create beneficial change in larger systems.

An effective nodal intervention restores connections that have been broken or creates new ones in order to move a system to its next level of health. Ideally, these connections facilitate existing flows of energy and resources, making them available for new purposes. For example, transit-oriented development seeks to concentrate new residences and commercial buildings in close proximity to transportation nodes. This reduces traffic and creates pedestrian-friendly districts, and at the same time it generates the housing density and foot traffic that allow commerce and cultural interactions to flourish.

The following suggestions are meant to help a design team think about their projects in terms of nodes.

Map the nodes. A designer who wishes to influence a particular system, for example a neighborhood, needs to assess the flows and exchanges occurring there. She will look first at what flows through, that is, at how the neighborhood is itself a node in a larger system. She will then focus down to a finer scale to understand what occurs within the neighborhood, identifying where linkages can be restored or created to lift it to a higher expression of its potential. This analysis is intended to reveal the nodes where a strategic intervention can be made. The nature of the node and the kind of intervention that it calls for then determines the characteristics that will need to be built into her project. If many different flows pass through the neighborhood, there will be a lot of energy to work with and the potential to influence a much larger arena or system.

Identify the right node for the intervention you want to make. Scale of flow is an important consideration with regard to both the volume of flows moving through a particular location and the potential influence they might exert within larger systems. People can easily be blinded by their own aspirations and enthusiasm. They will dedicate themselves to creating a small neighborhood park, imagine that it has the potential to leverage a whole city, and then wonder why they are having trouble attracting stakeholders from the larger system—when in fact their natural stakeholders are strictly local.

A regenerative practitioner will accurately assess the true relationship between a project and its larger environment and then tune his project's concept and strategies accordingly. A shop on a high-traffic pedestrian avenue offers other opportunities than one on a small backstreet. These are different kinds of nodes, and they speak to different audiences. To be both successful and transformative, a project needs to take each of them fully into account.

Choose the appropriate relationship with a node. It is also important to bear in mind that a high volume of flow is not always beneficial or benign. It can also be destructive. Think of the effects of a massive freeway system cutting through an old neighborhood or a flood moving through a minor river system. One important nodal effect is modulating a flow, slowing and distributing it or concentrating and intensifying it. In addition to preventing harm, this also creates opportunities for value-adding exchange.

Vibrant, artistic urban neighborhoods are almost never located in the high-rise financial and commercial centers of cities. They are found nearby, often in neighborhoods whose purposes have changed (for example, South of Market in San Francisco or Chelsea in Manhattan). A strong artisan community benefits from proximity to a major commercial center, but the centers themselves operate at too rapid a volume of exchange (and therefore too high a cost of real estate) to provide a hospitable environment for artists.

This phenomenon can also be seen in natural systems. In the late 1990s, Regenesis helped a couple plan a residence in the mountains of northern Arizona. The couple had identified what seemed to be the most dramatic and compelling place on their property and intended to locate their home there. The Regenesis team helped them see that this was a node in the landscape where the flows of wind, water, fire, cold air drainage, and wildlife traffic were concentrated. It was exciting to be sure, but not an ideal place to put a house. The couple ended up relocating the building site to a gentle slope within sight of their original choice. Two years later, when a devastating forest fire followed by monsoonal flooding destroyed all of the surrounding homes in the area, their home was completely unscathed.

ENDNOTES

1. Jaime Lerner, *Urban Acupuncture: Celebrating Principles of Change that Enrich City Life* (Washington, DC: Island Press, 2014) pp. 2–3.
2. Barry Commoner, *The Closing Circle: Nature, Man, and Technology* (New York: Alfred A. Knopf, Inc., 1971).
3. Henry R. Luce, "A Letter from the Publisher," *Time Magazine*, Vol. 95 No. 5, February 2, 1970.
4. Francis Pisani, "Networks as a Unifying Pattern of Life Involving Different Processes at Different Levels: An Interview with Fritjof Capra," *International Journal of Communication* 1, 2007, Feature 5-25 (accessed August 31, 2015) http://ijoc.org.
5. Fritjof Capra, "The Web of Life," Schrodinger Lecture Series, Trinity College, Dublin, 1977 (accessed August 31, 2015) www-users.york.ac.uk/~lsdc1/SysBiol/capra.weboflife.schrodingerlecture.1997.pdf.
6. Peter J. Marcotullio and Grant Boyle, editors, "Defining an Ecosystem Approach to Urban Management and Policy Development," UNU IAS Report (Tokyo: United Nations University Institute of Advanced Studies, Yokohama, 2003) (accessed August 31, 2015) http://collections.unu.edu/eserv/UNU:3109/UNUIAS_UrbanReport.pdf. Launched in 1971, UNESCO's Man and the Biosphere Program (MAB) is an Intergovernmental Scientific Program that aims to establish a scientific basis for the improvement of relationships between people and their environments. More information at www.unesco.org/new/en/natural-sciences/environment/ecological-sciences/man-and-biosphere-programme/.
7. Raymond J. Cole, Peter Busby, Robin Guenther, Leah Briney, Aiste Blaviesciunaite, and Tatiana Alencar, "A regenerative design framework: Setting new aspirations and initiating new discussions," *Building Research & Information*, 40:1, 2012.
8. Daniel Kemmis, *The Good City and the Good Life: Renewing the Sense of Community* (Boston: Houghton Mifflin Company, 1995).
9. Jaime Lerner, *Urban Acupuncture: Celebrating Pinpricks of Change that Enrich Life* (Washington, DC: Island Press, 2014).
10. Nicholas Mang, *Leadershhip Case Study of Curitiba, Brazil, in Towards a Regenerative Psychology of Urban Planning*, (San Francisco: Saybrook Graduate School and Research Center, May 2009) (accessed August 31, 2015) http://gradworks.umi.com/33/68/3368975.html.
11. Jaime Lerner, *Urban Acupuncture: Celebrating Pinpricks of Change that Enrich Life* (Washington, DC: Island Press, 2014).

CHAPTER 8

DEVELOPMENTAL WORK

> *Development is not a matter of how much one has*
> *but how much one can do with whatever one has.*[1]
>
> Russell Ackoff

Conventional projects start with a concept and ask how to manifest it within a system. Regenerative development projects start from the system's potential and use this as a basis for conceptualizing a project. This simple reversal carries with it a powerful implication: A project begins only when a community has engaged in dialogue about its own potential. From this dialogue, a field of caring can be generated, and within this field of caring, a project is able to step into a regenerative role.

A spirit of connection and caring is critical if diverse constituencies are to find a way to work together constructively. Without it, they can become entrenched and reactionary, even fighting to prevent changes that are beneficial for the community as a whole. Within a field of caring, diversity and disagreement can be assets, so long as they are informed by a sense of will and purpose.

This leads us to the premise that a project can only create systemic benefit within a field of caring, co-creativity, and co-responsibility.

Premise Eight: A project can only create systemic benefit within a field of caring, co-creativity, and co-responsibility.

AVOIDANCE BREEDS REACTIVITY

Developers who set out to "do good" are often shocked to encounter opposition from their communities. Yet it happens all the time. Much has been written about the Not-In-My-Backyard reaction of activists who organize to stop development in their neighborhoods. Whether NIMBY is seen as selfish and anti-progress or courageous depends on circumstance and perspective. Activists trying to prevent fracking or mining in their watershed might be viewed as environmental champions; or they might be accused of being impediments to a stable economy. Similarly, activists organizing to stop a homeless shelter from going into their neighborhood might seem selfish to some, pragmatic to others.

From a regenerative development perspective, the NIMBY problem doesn't arise from the motivations of activists. It comes from the fact that they are pushed into a posture of reactivity. In other words, they are almost always reacting to what appears to be an intrusion—for example, a developer with his own idea of what should be done with a particular piece of land. Even when the developer is also a member of the community, neighborhood residents often feel as if they are being pressured from the "outside."

While developers may blame this reactivity on activists, the fact is that conventional design processes are carefully managed to minimize any chance for proactive community involvement. While planning authorities generally require neighborhood notification and public input as a prerequisite for approval, developers often strive to limit community input as much as possible. When input is solicited, it usually takes the form of laying out a finished concept in the hopes of selling the community on it.

Even where community issues don't shut down a project outright, they tend to get resolved through negotiation and compromise rather than creative collaboration. This can erode the vision and viability of a project. For example, reducing densities can increase costs per unit, thus pricing out lower-income residents.

A CLASSIC LOSE-LOSE

In 2015, a city council meeting in Santa Fe, New Mexico, turned into a painful, six-hour ordeal. A team of local developers with a reputation for successful green and community-minded projects had come before the council to present its newest plan, unintentionally stirring up a firestorm of protest in the process.

Santa Fe is an attractive and culturally vibrant small city, but its steadily rising property values combined with low availability of rental housing have pushed younger and low- to middle-income families out. Although the city continues to attract the young artists and creatives that it needs to maintain its cachet as an art center, these transplants struggle to find a foothold and frequently move on to settle elsewhere. Local conversations about making the city more livable for young residents had been recurring for more than a decade, spinning off a variety of successful projects in arenas ranging from entrepreneurship to the music venues. Now, these developers were taking on another missing piece of the puzzle: affordable housing.

The developers proposed a residential complex geared toward young people seeking affordable living spaces to rent. It offered a mix of market-rate and subsidized units. In addition, the project embraced high sustainability aspirations. It was centrally located within the city, directly adjacent to the Santa Fe River along an established bus route and a planned extension to the city's growing network of bike paths. It included rainwater catchment, graywater reuse, community gardens, edible landscaping, river trail access, super-low energy use, and a pair of electric vehicles on site for a resident car-share. Not only was the development team addressing a serious, documented, and much-talked-about need in the community; it was aiming to do so in a way that embodied the city's progressive values and sustainability aspirations.

The team had asked for a zoning variance because the objective of providing affordable rents required higher density than was currently allowed. They considered this a reasonable request because the increase was modest, and moderate densification would bring certain community benefits. However, upon learning that the project would increase density, the neighborhood erupted, organizing the city's network of neighborhood associations to oppose the project.

Although the project site was in the center of town, less than a quarter-mile from the city's largest commercial corridor, it had once been a thriving agricultural area and still had a strong identity as such. In addition to single-family residences, the area was home to a native-plants nursery and a community farm. The development site, itself, had formerly been a center for teaching sustainable agriculture.

Many of the families in the area had been there for generations. The neighboring village, which had been inhabited continuously since the mid-1600s, was designated a Traditional Historic Community. Although current zoning would have allowed a complex of almost the same density that the developers were proposing, the city's General Plan, which had been developed with strong neighborhood input over 15 years, stated the intention that the area maintains its semi-rural character, with a density of one unit per acre. This gray area between what the current zoning allowed—or almost allowed—and what the community preferred became a breeding ground for intense frustration and debate.

The council meeting had a powerfully polarizing effect. Neighborhood groups from around the city spoke out against a project that was so strongly opposed by its neighbors, arguing that it would disrupt local identity. They warned against setting a dangerous precedent in a city with a strong legacy of protecting and celebrating its historic roots. Advocates for efforts to retain young people argued that a rejection of the project would only continue to push development further and further out of the city's core. Their point was that the critical needs of the city as a whole should matter more than the concerns of just one neighborhood. Public testimony on both sides was heated, personal, and polarized around age differences.

In the end, after more than six hours of input and just past midnight, the council voted unanimously to reject the project. In general, the governing body agreed that such a project was critically needed, but that to allow it to be developed in this particular location would be a violation of the community's trust. In doing so, they were left facing a tangle of questions about how to grow the city in a way that meets the needs of all of its residents without undermining its core character. Additionally, many of those who came to the public input session left feeling strongly alienated from the civic process.

The developers were taken aback by the opposition they encountered. They had worked for years in good faith to address a real and acknowledged community need. They had attempted to balance the costs of the land with design solutions that would meet the needs of renters while being acceptable to the community. They had engaged in a campaign to share their vision with the neighborhood, reached out to community leaders, and worked hard to inspire the young people who would benefit from the project. In the end, they had invested so much of their own capital to bring the project to this stage, that when it was rejected they chose to abandon it rather than risk more. It was a classic case of lose-lose.

PROACTIVE VERSUS CO-CREATIVE

When developers *do* attempt to engage communities proactively, they usually end up with a tangle of opinions and issues that stifle their ability to be creative themselves. Activities like group visioning and brainstorming often yield long laundry lists of likes and dislikes, wants and dreams, opinions and beliefs. These incoherent collections of contradictory viewpoints are rarely useful. Developers struggle to find the relevance of this input to their projects, and more often than not it ends up on a shelf somewhere, leaving residents feeling dissatisfied or even betrayed by the process.

The problem is that stakeholders are not invited into an authentic *co-creative* process. Thinking creatively as an individual is not the same as engaging with others to think together. Co-creative work requires a structured process that is oriented in a common direction. Unlike brainstorming, which scatters thinking, it brings focus and discipline to group process.

When community members engage co-creatively, they develop a real stake in the outcome of a project. In other words, they become *co-responsible* for the project's success. As responsible agents, they show up. A developer with the option to engage a collaborative community rather than convince hostile neighbors, seek endorsements, and rally special-interest groups is much more likely to succeed.

DEVELOPMENTAL PROCESSES

Regenerative development is not about finding a magic formula that will solve the world's problems. Rather, it enables communities to evolve beyond current conditions by growing capabilities that they don't already possess. Put another way, regenerative development is *developmental*. It builds the capability of the systems it affects (such as organizations, communities, and watersheds) to serve as catalysts for continuing co-evolution.

The successful completion of a regenerative project is actually a beginning, not an end. It launches an ongoing process that requires local players to be both able and willing to continue collaborating into the future. It is only through such ongoing collaboration that the full potential of the project is realized. A foundation for growing the necessary understanding, skills, and capabilities is laid in the design process. This is why regenerative development gives as much attention to the design of the *process* as to the *product* it delivers.

A developmental design process works directly on growing meaning and will. It starts with building strong relationships among stakeholders (including the members of the project team) around a shared identity and future. It continues by helping stakeholders envision the roles they are called to play in order to bring this future into being. It supports the relationships, new capabilities, and self-accountability that these roles will require.

The work of a designer is to create a process that invites everyone into this co-learning culture. Project teams seek to develop their capability to think and act more systemically. Local stakeholders are invited into a field of commitment and caring where they can step forward as co-designers and ongoing stewards. Local institutions and ecosystems are seen as project beneficiaries, and improving their ability to do their work is an explicit project goal.

Thus, the eighth fundamental principle of regenerative development is to *design the design process to be developmental* for all stakeholders.

Principle Eight: Design the design process to be developmental.

ALBUQUERQUE'S INTERNATIONAL DISTRICT

Albuquerque's east mesa forms a high alluvial plain that overlooks the city's historic downtown, located along the Rio Grande. The mesa's dry grasslands were used mostly for grazing during the city's first 200 years. Near the turn of the twentieth century, homesteaders ventured into the area, followed by settlers in the years following World War II. Among these settlers were black homesteaders who developed the city's first suburban neighborhood to welcome black and other non-white families.

America's storied highway, Route 66, ran right through the middle of the east mesa. In the mid-twentieth century it sprouted a vibrant commercial strip to serve the throngs of tourists and travelers who began to explore the American West. By 1970, Interstate 40 had replaced the old US 66, and three nearby military air bases had merged and developed on-base housing for personnel. East Mesa residential populations decreased, businesses and motels were abandoned, empty houses torn down, and weeds overgrew the vacant lots.

Into this underutilized district a new wave of immigrants began to settle. They included refugees from Asia, Africa, and Latin America, fleeing war or violence in their countries of origin, who were moved into the neighborhood by the city. Cheap housing also attracted drug traffickers, which brought in other unstable populations, including gang members, and raised the neighborhood crime rate. The cultural mix was lively (more than 30 languages were spoken in the local schools) but also volatile, and the poverty of the district helped fuel an extended period of violent crime. The neighborhood became known by the tabloid title "The War Zone."

In the late 1980s a group of local advocates stood up for the neighborhood and carried out a courageous campaign to rid it of its crime and the hated nickname. They organized themselves across neighborhoods, primarily through neighborhood associations, and in 2009, after many years of effort, successfully petitioned city, county, and state officials to designate them the International District. The intention was to help alter perceptions of the area by celebrating its unique assets, including a host of international restaurants, shops, and cultural venues that could serve as a destination for people around the state. Yet, despite these efforts, the community continued to struggle with internal and external perceptions that it is a war zone.

In local discussions, many hard questions arose. What is required to alter the general perception of a place? What would it mean to further "live into" this place as the International District? What changes would have to be made? How could the new perception be passed on to younger generations? How could it be written into the landscape and built environment?

In 2011, Nicholas Mang and Christy Snyder from the Story of Place Institute (SOPI) began to work with International District community members. Together with the University of New Mexico School of Architecture and Planning, Littleglobe (a New Mexico–based nonprofit committed to interdisciplinary collaborative art projects), the City of Albuquerque's Cultural Services Department, and the Albuquerque Metropolitan Arroyo Flood Control Authority, they began to work with residents

> . . . in a collaborative process of storytelling, art and design toward the ultimate goals of (1) building positive perception and identity, (2) transforming outdoor spaces through creative placemaking projects, and (3) nurturing cross-sector community relationships and catalyzing community-led development efforts.[2]

Although their overarching objective was to find leveraged projects that would advance their goals, they had no preconceptions about what these projects would be. Instead, to reveal them they relied on a process for evoking the collective intelligence of the community.

SOPI launched the project with research that explored the natural and social history of the district, including its current dynamics and aspirations. The team walked the area with community members and held in-depth conversations with residents, natural scientists, urban planners, and local historians. This interview process represented a "kind of total immersion in the social and ecological systems at play." To carry out this purpose, Christy Snyder moved into the neighborhood and lived there for three months.

SOPI shared what it was learning as it went along, promoting a collective exploration of the character of the district and its potential—"what it is at its best"—as reflected in residents' dreams for its future. Community members were invited into a conscious articulation of the stake they held in their place and awakened to a sense of purpose that felt worthy to them.

From here it became possible to convene local gatherings to share findings and explore ways to light a few sparks in order to energize the whole system. SOPI's first effort was a street festival, called ID LIVE!, which celebrated the neighborhood's diverse cultural wealth (Figures 8.1 through 8.3). Then the team went on to explore more ambitious and enduring projects. One idea was an international market with a flexible, "pop-up" infrastructure to allow for mobile food trucks and vendor kiosks, which would enable local small entrepreneurs to participate.

FIGURE 8.1 A local crowd gathers at the ID LIVE! festival.
Copyright © Story of Place Institute, Inc.

FIGURE 8.2 Residents converse at the ID LIVE! festival.

Copyright © Story of Place Institute, Inc.

FIGURE 8.3 Street performance at the ID LIVE! festival.

Copyright © Story of Place Institute, Inc.

A second was to restart an existing community land trust to manage the many abandoned properties still found in the district. Chartered to use the spaces flexibly, the trust serves to establish temporary or portable micro-housing for new immigrants, for example, or create community gardens or more permanent housing. Its role is to act as a bridge to assist low-income families, including many refugee families, in their efforts to become established members of the community.

A third idea led to a "story curation" program, in partnership with the New Mexico Humanities Council. It collected the cultural history of the district in the form of residents' stories for the purpose of countering the negative associations of the "war zone." SOPI had discovered that many local champions, even those most committed to shifting public perceptions, still unconsciously framed their stories in terms of war. The team sought a more well-rounded narrative, one that could reconnect local people to their "historical cultural, ecological, and economic patterns of place, and from this basis develop a shared vision for the future that . . . lifts people's spirits and gives them renewed hope for developing a better, healthier life for themselves, their children and grandchildren."[3]

The fourth idea was a "Story Plaza Garden," where this narrative could be expressed. Collectively designed by neighborhood residents, the garden would be a gathering place for festivals, markets, and outdoor concerts; the garden would also be designed to host dynamic, rotating story "exhibits" and public art installations to support ongoing creative expression. Upon completion, it would serve as a new anchor and gateway for the district, one of a string of such neighborhood centers along Albuquerque's Route 66.

UPGRADING THE PREDESIGN PROCESS

The International District shares qualities with many other creative place-making projects. Essentially, these projects avoid the developer-community polarization by enabling communities to charter their own development. They start with a predesign process that invites residents to think about and celebrate their community's potential before jumping into land-use decisions.

Private development projects can upgrade their predesign processes by borrowing this page from the creative place-making book. While predesign is usually dedicated to due diligence, it would be better used to build stakeholder alignment. This reframes the purpose of public conversation. Instead of putting the project at the center, which invites reactivity, it puts the common wealth of place and community at the center. Shared purpose, articulated before any design work begins, creates a field of energy that is entirely different from the public brawls that many development projects encounter. When the time comes to design the project, a stakeholder alliance is already in place.

Predesign can be used to establish several important patterns that will influence or carry through all subsequent phases of the project. For example, the work to discover the potential and identify the vocation of a place establishes a strong collaborative bond with key stakeholders. This work is inherently challenging, for project team and community members alike, and requires a high degree of introspection, authenticity, reflective engagement, and capacity for integration and synthesis. In other words, it requires a working atmosphere that is almost the opposite of a politically divisive public hearing.

A public hearing fosters reactivity because it frames the relationship between project and community in terms of separation. Members of the public are essentially invited to contribute narrow and self-interested opinions. By contrast, a developmental process purposefully engages the aspirations of the participants, inviting the kind of genuine listening and understanding from which relationships of mutual respect can develop.

As a result of this process, it becomes possible to identify and recruit the members of the guild, which will further the larger systemic changes that are desired. Each member enters the process with the understanding that the guild, collectively, is trying to accomplish something that hasn't been done before and will require that she develop herself, personally. The integration of personal and collective development helps grow a culture of mutual support, accountability, and forbearance. The more ambitious the calling, the more committed the partners, the greater the opportunity for profound transformation at all levels of the system.

LAS SALINAS, VIÑA DEL MAR, CHILE

Viña del Mar is a garden city located on the Pacific Coast of Chile. Once a thriving port and a jewel of enlightened urban design, in the late twentieth century it experienced decades of decline and disinvestment. Yet buried in the collective memory of the community was a strong sense of what it had been (Figures 8.4 through 8.6).

For the past 10 years, a real estate group called Las Salinas had been master planning a new campus of residential high rises on a 40-acre brownfield site, a former oil tank farm in the southwestern part of the city. Las Salinas is a small division within one of the largest corporations in Chile, a conglomerate with businesses in gasoline, forestry, and fishing. The corporation was strongly disliked by Viña del Mar community groups, who universally referred to it as "the enemy."

FIGURE 8.4 A view of the horizon in Viña del Mar, Chile.
Copyright © Regenesis Group, Inc. Photo by Tim Murphy.

FIGURE 8.5 Street art in Viña del Mar, Chile.
Copyright © Regenesis Group, Inc. Photo by Tim Murphy.

FIGURE 8.6 A panoramic view of a park in Viña del Mar, Chile.
Copyright © Regenesis Group, Inc. Photo by Tim Murphy.

Las Salinas could see that even if it submitted a master plan for the project, it was likely facing 15 years of lawsuits that would carry it all the way to the Chilean Supreme Court. There was no assurance that the company would win, and Las Salinas' CEO thought it wasn't a good bet. Sasaki Associates, the lead architectural planners for the project, was aware of Regenesis and its work on community reconciliation. The planning team mentioned the idea of reconciliation to the owners, and it caught their attention. They brought in Regenesis to help with community engagement.

In its first visit, the Regenesis team met with the firm responsible for public relations with all of the activist groups. The meeting unrolled like a war room strategy session. "How are we going to placate this group? What can we do to reduce the influence of that group?" The Regenesis team pulled the CEO aside and asked him, "Why are you involved in this project?"

He replied, "Although real estate development is not our core business, we care about this community. We've been given much by our country and we want to give something back to this town." When it was pointed out that this sounded more like a campaign for battle than a gift, he responded, "Yeah, I guess we need to change how we're going about this."

One by one, Regenesis met the local activist groups, who would invariably open by saying, "Oh, so *you* are with the enemy." "Yes," the team answered, "but *our* focus is on the city." This response disarmed the activists, who willingly shared their perspectives on what the city had been and what it could be again. The result was magical. In the first three weeks of engagement, 18 key groups shifted from extreme opposition to neutrality or strong support for the project. In group after group a sense of participation and potential had been awakened.

Activists realized, with some relief, that they had been fighting over one small piece of land, only because they had given up hope. In their minds, this was the game they could play, for the rest of the city was already dead. When they saw that they could use their considerable energies to shift the direction of the city as a whole and that they could partner with the project to accomplish this, they responded with enthusiasm. Speaking on behalf of his group, one stakeholder commented, "We want to be part of this. It's the first time we've been able to dream in thirty years."

At the same time, Regenesis was at work with the project team. In a parallel process, Las Salinas also became aware of the potential to restore the vitality of Viña del Mar. Suddenly, at the end of three weeks, the developers and the local communities discovered themselves in a totally unexpected relationship of shared aspiration and strong commitment. At the moment of epiphany, the project manager recognized that he had been asked to move from a transactional relationship with the community to one of reciprocity. Viña del Mar was already transformed, and the project had not even broken ground.

Building from this strong beginning, the next steps in the process have been to work with the activist groups to envision the future they want to pursue. Regenesis co-generated principles with them to help overcome their history of divisiveness and guide their future work together. Most recently, the Regenesis team has introduced developmental frameworks to help them become more systemic and strategic in their thinking.

As an interesting side note, Regenesis had to learn culturally appropriate ways of communicating with both the citizens of Viña del Mar and the Chilean project team. Chile is sometimes called the "Switzerland of Latin America." Chileans can be procedural to a fault: Nothing exists unless it has been documented. For the community activists, the Regenesis team laid out a comprehensive roadmap for the design process—how it was going to work, what it was going to accomplish, and how that intersected with their dreams of a regenerated city—a form of transparency that they found deeply meaningful.

For the Las Salinas team, Regenesis created a graph that showed the starting position of each of the stakeholder groups and where they had progressed, ranging from neutral to strongly supportive. Seeing this shift in graph form powerfully communicated to the Chilean managers, in a way that anecdotal stories never could have, that the approach was effective and worth continuing.

LIMITATIONS OF CONVENTIONAL APPROACHES

Designers and developers have become understandably protective of their planning efforts. They operate in a hostile battle zone of environmental activists, adversarial regulators, and angry neighborhood watchdog groups. Fear of disruption, loss of control, and excess costs lead many project managers to focus primarily on keeping the process efficient. Inviting the public in is tantamount to inviting a fox into the chicken coop. Public input is generally seen as a nuisance, to be integrated into the final plan based on a calculus of how badly it will impact the project and how great the threat of opposition actually is.

Not surprisingly, this protectiveness gets interpreted as secretiveness and ill intent, with the end result of increased hostility because it prevents or inhibits public involvement. It also encourages excessive dependence on specialist expertise to justify a project's existence. Still, development professionals find it difficult to move off of this embattled terrain for fear that trying something new will only make the situation more costly in terms of time and money.

Writing about his work in the International District, Nicholas Mang points out that:

> When planning's overriding goal is one of functioning efficiency, there is a tendency to seek to eliminate perturbations to the process. We want the process to go as smoothly as possible, which is understandable. The danger, however, is when this desire leads to highly controlled, non-participatory processes that engage civic stakeholders in only a token fashion, thus creating buffers to authentic engagement and co-creation in the community. This leads to a process that is too constrictive and top down, thereby diminishing the potential for creative, holistic solutions. It also tends to lead to an increasingly disenfranchised populace who feel less and less a sense of ownership and stewarding role in their community.[4]

Shifting from a limited and closely managed process to one that is genuinely participatory is challenging. But the challenges tend to be personal, rather than technical. As Barbara Batshalom, founder of the Sustainable Performance Institute, points out, "The difficulty of this process is that it challenges people's ability to go outside of their comfort zone, do things differently, and refine their personal skills when encountering resistance and conflict."[5] Working regeneratively requires alignment and strong commitment from the entire project team, as well as periodic reinforcement to keep that alignment and commitment alive.

Still, this is where the professional disciplines, planning, and design, are headed. In his book *The Art of City Making*, Charles Landry predicts that:

> Planning is about to be different from what it used to be—it is set to be a more holistic process. . . . The shift from "participation in planning"

where you merely consult to "participatory planning" where you involve will get us beyond the knee-jerk consultation processes so common yet unempowering. The planning professions should see this moment as an opportunity for them.[6]

GUIDELINES FOR APPLYING THE PRINCIPLE

The following guidelines can help a design team find its sea legs when it comes to working with local stakeholders developmentally.

Start with a collective process to discover potential. The principle *work from potential not problems* is particularly critical in the predesign process. The Santa Fe developers started with a community-wide problem (lack of afford-able housing) and invested enormous resources in laying out their solution to it. Failure to engage the neighborhood in a dialogue about its own potential created an atmosphere of reactivity rather than a field of mutual caring. This reinforced the perception that the project was an outsider with its own agenda. In a sense, the developers were blinded by their own good intentions and thus doomed from the start.

Create an "equation of co-responsibility." This requires extending the purview of a project so that it can actually affect whole systems, because it is around these that it is appropriate to ask stakeholders to take responsibility. Participatory design is often mistaken for asking the public to comment on or make suggestions about a project. But, in fact, it is participation in the design of the public sphere. When stakeholders are aligned around a common purpose that is large enough in scope to bind them all together, then the project can join with them, shoulder to shoulder, as an ally in that purpose. Relationships become collegial, each stakeholder contributing to the collective, systemic understanding of the potential of place and then applying that understanding in their own work.

Approach design as a reciprocal developmental process. Preconceived solutions have no place in regeneration. It is the spirit of a place that we seek to regenerate. This requires a truly open process on the part of the design and development team, one in which expertise has the humility to place itself in service to inquiry. Vision and planning grow out of the understanding that comes from ongoing community dialogue.

Make the core values of the project explicit and shared, and use them as a source of creativity. Many of the conflicts that arise around projects come from locking down on elements that are "non-negotiable." This is a clear indication that thinking has become rigid and creativity has stopped. At this point it is necessary to return to the core values that are the source of inspiration and partnership among participants, and use them as the basis for reconciliation. This lifts the work of both the project team and the community stakeholders to higher levels of creativity.

Employ new measures of success. Regenerative goals redefine what's at stake from protecting what *is* to pursuing *what could be*. This provides a basis for developing a shared sense of what success means and therefore how it should be measured. For example, a primary indicator might be how well a community is able to balance the development of all five forms of capital. (See Chapter 4, page 95.)

Identify or invent the portfolio of design tools and technologies that are appropriate to the unique character of a place. One of the most common questions people ask when presented with a new approach is, "Can you show me a place where this has worked?" At the same time, communities are often skeptical of approaches brought in from the outside, and it is equally common to hear, "Well, that might have worked in Albany (or Missoula or Bogota) but we're different. It won't work here."

What this expresses is a nearly universal desire to be seen and respected as individual and unique. No one really wants to be a statistic. The resolution of this contradiction is to co-invent an approach that is native to the soil of a place. This requires using the credibility and expertise earned through professional experience to privilege *not knowing* over knowing. It can be hard as seasoned professionals to give up having all the right answers, but that is the only way to discover new answers.

A significant side benefit of the development of unique, place-specific solutions and practices is the enrichment it brings to the sustainability field.

Monocultures of thought and technology are just as brittle in the face of environmental disturbance as monocultures of corn in a farm field. As leading sustainability thinker Wolfgang Sachs has observed, "After all, it is only from places that variety crops up, because it is in places that people weave the present into their particular thread of history."[7]

ENDNOTES

1. Russell Ackoff, "Transforming the Systems Movement," opening speech at the Third International Conference on Systems Thinking in Management (ICSTM '04), May 26, 2004 (accessed March 17, 2016) www.acasa.upenn.edu/RLAConfPaper.pdf
2. Nicholas Mang and Christy Snyder, *Story of Place: The International District*, A year-one report as part of the NEA "Our Town" funded Stories of Route 66: The International District Project. December 31, 2014.
3. Ibid.
4. Ibid.
5. Barbara Batshalom, "Everyone is practicing integrative design . . . at least that's what they say," in Bill Reed and 7group, *The Integrative Design Guide to Green Building: Refining the Practice of Sustainability* (Hoboken, NJ: John Wiley & Sons, Inc., 2009).
6. Charles Landry, *The Art of City Making* (London: Earthscan, 2006).
7. Wolfgang Sachs, editor, *The Development Dictionary: A Guide to Knowledge as Power* (London: Zed Books, 1992).

PART THREE

BECOMING A REGENERATIVE CHANGE AGENT

To be agents of transformation, designers must transform themselves. They must redesign their own thinking and ways of being. In other words, regenerative development requires inner work. Over time, a regenerative practitioner learns to observe herself and manage her state of being in service to the causes she cares about. She develops the ability to work creatively with ambiguity and uncertainty, which enables her to welcome the complexity of natural systems and the diversity of perspective that characterizes living communities. Thus, she becomes a systems actualizer. The benefits accrue not only to her professional practice but also to her personal life.

*The most meaningful activity in which a human being can be engaged is
one that is directly related to human evolution.*[1]

Jonas Salk

Beatrice Benne, a Bay Area–based community development practitioner, has a
passionate interest in complexity science and living systems theory (Figure E.1).
Her work has spanned organizational development, business education,
and urban development, all of which she sees as integral to the evolution
of healthy communities. She became interested in regenerative work as the
result of the realization that organizations, networks, and communities are
all living systems. This transformed her understanding of the world and her
sense of who she would need to become in order to have a beneficial impact.

FIGURE E.1 Beatrice Benne is a Bay Area–based community
developer with a regenerative practice.

She recognized early in her career that evolving social and organizational systems would require evolving herself and the people she encounters in her
work. As she puts it:

> In order to evolve systems we need to develop the people within those
> systems. The two go together; they are totally integrated. To meet the
> challenges facing us at this time in history, we need to increase the ability
> of the systems that we create to deal with complexity. As we do that, we
> also need to develop our capacity to embrace more complexity so that
> we can operate these complex systems effectively. It's not development
> in the abstract, but through the work itself.

After some years of testing different aspects of the theory, Benne had an opportunity to facilitate a regenerative planning process in a small community in Brittany, France—a place she described as "crying out for healing." Located in an especially beautiful region, with a high concentration of megalithic sites, the community had experienced several generations of decline. Houses stood vacant, alcoholism was rampant, and the village had become little more than a residential outpost of larger, nearby towns (Figure E.2).

FIGURE E.2 A coastal view in Brittany, France.

Into this situation, a native resident had envisioned a redevelopment process, regenerating small-scale agriculture and artisanal businesses, linked to a network of ecological villages throughout France. For this purpose, a group of design practitioners had gathered to explore the potential for his project, and to help him understand the larger systems it could beneficially affect (Figure E.3).

FIGURE E.3 Participants at the workshop facilitated by Beatrice Benne.

Benne was astonished at how powerfully inspirational the process was for participants, and how quickly they were able to grasp and utilize complex living frameworks. More important, she was able to observe what was required in herself to enable this nature of community process. As she reported later:

> Finally, I figured out that my own state of being was critical to creating the right environment for breakthroughs. I needed to be open and caring and grounded, and I needed to invite the group into the same space. I had to hold in mind the potential that lay behind this little village. That changed the tone of the entire interaction.

> For me, this work is fundamentally spiritual, although we don't speak much about that dimension. I was carried through the process in Brittany, as though there were some purpose beyond me. My challenge was to surrender and let go. The strategies didn't come from me or from the group I was working with. They came from the profound need and possibility of the place. Of course, that meant setting our egos aside and listening deeply to what wanted to come into the world. And that requires total commitment to personal development.

Note

A vast literature has grown up around the subject of human development, encompassing psychology, philosophy, and spirituality. One could say that growing ourselves into the people we aspire to be is what defines us as human beings. The following chapter introduces a few simple ideas that may be especially useful to someone who chooses to become a regenerative practitioner. The ideas are built around the notion that designers can be systems actualizers, and that this is a powerful context within which to grow oneself.

▮ ENDNOTE

1. Jonas Salk, *Anatomy of Reality: Merging of Intuition and Reality*, Convergence Series (Santa Barbara, California: Praeger Publishers, Inc., 1985).

CHAPTER 9

SYSTEMS ACTUALIZING

Sustainability is an inside job...[1]
Kathia Laszlo

Regenerative development cultivates evolutionary capacity in projects and living communities. This creates outcomes that are harmonious with the livingness of the world, but it also means that regenerative development can't be reduced to a recipe or formula. It must be reinvented for each new project and for each new situation.

This places high demands on regenerative practitioners, who can never settle into the comfort of having "the answers." The state of "not knowing" that is necessary for true innovation requires steadiness of being and clarity of purpose. In a world that demands certainty, regenerative practitioners must break old habits of thought. In other words, just as regenerative development invites communities to change themselves, it invites designers to change themselves as well.

INNER WORK

Regenerative development is grounded in a belief that we cannot make the outer transformations we envision for the world without making inner transformations in how we think and who we are able to be. The focus of this inner work is to evolve ourselves. It emphasizes the necessary growth in thinking and being that is required to successfully undertake regenerative projects.

Inner work is personal, energized by the innate human drive to grow and develop. It addresses an inner landscape of being, rather than outer landscapes of place. For this reason, it is often overlooked, discounted, or pursued for personal enrichment rather than as part of professional practice. It is rarely integrated into the workplace. Yet evolving what we design and how we collaborate depends ultimately on who we are as we work.

SELF AND SYSTEMS ACTUALIZING

Inner work is often equated with psychologist Abraham Maslow's concept of *self-actualization*, which he defined as "the desire for self-fulfillment" and the drive "to become everything that one is capable of becoming."[2]

Prior to Maslow's formulation, psychology was primarily focused on helping people deal with mental disorders. In other words, it was a problem-solving approach. Humanistic psychology brought holism to human development, based on the premise that there is no inherent limit to human potential. Its goal was a "fully growing and self-fulfilling human being . . . in whom all his potentialities are coming to full development, the one whose inner nature expresses itself freely."[3]

From a regenerative development perspective, self-actualization is a critical aspect of inner work. However, it is not—and cannot be—the goal. In fact, emphasis on self alone can isolate us from the larger living systems we are part of and the value-adding role we have to play within them. As Nicholas Mang writes, "Without this larger systems awareness, we act and perceive as independent entities without an inner appreciation or caring for the collective living systems that source us and bind us together."[4] Or, in the words of James Hillman, "We're working on our relationships constantly, and our feelings and reflections, but look what's left out of that. . . . What's left out is a deteriorating world."[5]

In order to anchor self-actualizing work in a way that serves the world outside us, we must incorporate an additional layer, the psychology of what might be called *systems actualization*. As individuals, we live in a world of systems. Although we are often unconscious of their influence, we work with them, on them, and in them. Every "self" is nested within a system and is dependent upon developing some level of reciprocal nurturance with that system. Failure to take this reciprocity into account can profoundly constrain our efforts to self-actualize.

This leads to the ninth fundamental premise of regenerative development: *The actualization of a self requires the simultaneous development of the systems of which it is a part.*

Premise Nine: The actualization of a self requires the simultaneous development of the systems of which it is a part.

Developing a system goes beyond setting it up or even maintaining it. Rather, development unveils the inherent potential in a system and moves it toward actualization in an ongoing, evolutionary way. In a living, regenerating world, the self we need to actualize is a systems-actualizing self.

For this reason, the ninth principle of regenerative development is to *become a systems actualizer.*

Principle Nine: Become a systems actualizer.

BECOMING A SYSTEMS ACTUALIZER

A regenerative practitioner looks beyond her own actualization in order to understand the systems that support life where she lives and discover her value-adding role in nurturing their ongoing capacity to grow and evolve. This work does not replace self-actualizing; it extends it. Just as we cannot think about self-actualizing outside of the context of systems, working on systems actualization requires that we become self-actualizing individuals.

Just as we cannot think about self-actualizing outside of the context of systems, working on systems actualization requires that we become self-actualizing individuals.

Becoming a steward for the evolution of a whole provides a practitioner with an enlarged context for expressing her unique potential and offers guidance for what she must develop to fully realize that potential. It requires capabilities beyond those traditionally taught in educational institutions or professional development programs. These include the will to cross the boundaries that prevent innovation, the dexterity of thinking needed to integrate increasingly complex systems within our purview, and the ability to manage our state as we work. Setting developmental aims is one way to grow these meta-capabilities.

DEVELOPMENTAL AIMS

An *aim* helps us to hold an internal pattern through time so that we are able to maintain an appropriate state of being and quality of thinking, regardless of changing circumstances. The art of archery demonstrates the concept of aim. An archer has a goal, the target that she wants her arrow to strike. To hit that mark, she needs to hold the right pattern of relationships in her mind and body. These include how she employs her muscles, how tightly she stretches the bowstring, where she points the bow, and how she manages her breath and mental state. Mastering each of these requires years of practice and experience. The totality of these carefully developed relationships, their internal pattern, is her aim.

An aim defines what we are seeking to become in order to accomplish our goals. The importance of creating an aim comes from the recognition that who we are able to be in a given situation has an important influence on what we can create and, therefore, it helps determine what is possible.

By means of an aim, we stabilize our state of being so that we are less likely to become a victim of circumstance and more likely to hit the targets that we are shooting for. The ability to self-manage—to avoid collapsing into counterproductive states of being and habits of thinking—is a necessary prerequisite to becoming a systems actualizer.

The following aims lay out an inner path for anyone who wishes to become a regenerative practitioner. They are open ended, reflecting the lifelong developmental nature of this work. They are also invitations into ways of being that can have a profound influence on the nature of work that we are able to pursue and the collaborations that we are able to sustain.

AIM ONE: AWAKEN CARING

Anyone who has worked on generating new patterns of behavior for himself knows that will, when it is present, can be a powerful ally. Antoine de Saint-Exupéry beautifully conveyed this thought when he wrote, "If you want to build a ship, don't herd people together to collect wood and don't assign them tasks and work, but rather teach them to long for the endless immensity of the sea."[6] People have always celebrated in songs and stories those heroes who demonstrated the will to overcome great challenges in order to make a difference in the world. These stories remind us that human will, when connected to an important purpose, is an inexhaustible source of energy and creativity. Tapping this source, for ourselves and for the communities we serve, is essential if we are to become systems actualizers. The key to doing so is to awaken caring.

Fields of Caring

Many change efforts are mobilized in response to an impending crisis, but die away once the problem is solved. Systems actualization, by contrast, is fueled by seeing new potential and feeling called to bring it into being, to care enough to make it real. Because potential has no inherent limit, the changes that result from realizing one level will always reveal further levels that are yet to be realized.

Creating an energy field that evokes caring requires the inner capacity to see through existing circumstances to the potential reality that lies behind them. It then requires the faith that this deeper reality, in spite of all evidence to the contrary, is what longs to become manifest. As designers, it takes humility and ruthless honesty to engage in the deep listening that will reveal what is true about a place, rather than be seduced by fantasies of what it could be. Tapping into true potential is what gives us the ability to generate a field of caring, an energy field that can awaken an entire community.

Energy Fields

Fields of energy are all around us and, depending on the situation, might be characterized as uplifting or depressing, coalescing or fragmenting. One way to grasp what is meant by "energy field" is to consider the atmosphere in a restaurant. Restaurants can be cozy, elegant, bright, lively, subdued, cheesy, hip, creepy. Successful restaurateurs do a lot of thinking about how to create the right field for the kind of customers and eating patterns that fit their business models (fast turnover versus leisurely dining, for example). Depending on their skill, they are able to sustain these fields through the ways they translate their overall intentions into the menu, the décor, the acoustics of the space, or the attitude of the staff.

Some fields are generated by physical energies such as wind, water, sunshine, or traffic. Sociological fields arise from cultural phenomena such as the colors people wear and whether or not there are pedestrians thronging the streets of a town. Fields can be vitalizing or devitalizing, depending on how well they lift the spirit of a community and what this spirit is directed toward. Taken together, these fields shape our experience and set limits to what it is possible to pursue.

If we are unconscious of their effects, energy fields manage us. Without our realizing it, they influence how we think, what we think about, and even what we value. By learning to consciously observe and reshape fields, we become able to take charge of our individual and collective destinies. One could say that regeneration begins when a field of vitalizing energy is intentionally introduced as the context for an activity. We experience this as a feeling of aliveness, a sense of hope that something meaningful can be created, and a commitment to participating in this creation. This is important because changing how we inhabit Earth is going to require significant shifts in thinking and behavior on the part of communities around the globe. Exhortations and regulations are the least efficient and, ultimately, most spirit-killing ways to create change.

One could say that regeneration begins when a field of vitalizing energy is intentionally introduced as the context for an activity.

A field of caring is inherently vitalizing. When it is present, it isn't necessary to cajole people to get them to cooperate. Instead, they see their destinies as linked to evolving health and potential for the whole. By working intentionally on creating the right field, a systems actualizer enhances the effectiveness of other sustainability and community development efforts. This is how communities generate the will to take charge of their own evolutions.

AIM TWO: HONOR COMPLEXITY

Much of the Western scientific and intellectual tradition has been built around the idea of atomization. If we can discover the smallest particle, then we can understand how the universe is built. If we can break problems into their component and, by implication, simpler parts, then we can more easily solve them. If we can isolate an object of study, limiting any variables that might influence it from the outside, then we can come to know it.

This atomizing bias makes Western cultures poorly equipped to comprehend living systems. Working with complex wholes is simply not part of the way we've been educated. Paula Underwood Spencer, a Native American and keeper of the Oneida tradition, offers an alternative possibility.

> The distinction that I want to make between Western science and the approach to science which my tradition, and perhaps other Native traditions, have found useful . . . is that first you look at the Forest . . . and *then* you look at the Path. . . . you first acquire an intuitive, whole understanding, and then you focus on a Specificity and examine it, and then you *always* put it *back* into the Whole.[7]

Living systems tend to become increasingly complex through time. When humans simplify nature to better manage it (for example, with monoculture farms), we betray not only reality but our own creative possibilities. Becoming a systems actualizer requires the opposite, embracing complexity rather than fighting it.

Living systems tend to become increasingly complex through time. When humans simplify nature . . . we betray not only reality but our own creative possibilities.

Culturally Determined Seeing

Honoring complexity as a source of life and creativity calls for adopting a new way of thinking, which includes shifting between foreground and background as needed. This ability, it turns out, is limited by cultural patterns, as demonstrated by experimental psychologist Richard Nisbett in research that he describes in *The Geography of Thought.* Working with 50 graduate students, half born in the United States, the other half raised in China, he conducted tests using a device for tracking eye movement.

Each student was shown a series of pictures on a computer. The pictures all featured a large foreground object, such as a tiger or a car, against a fairly complex, realistic background. Students were shown an image for three seconds, and then asked to refocus on a small cross on a white screen.

A consistent pattern emerged. The American students' eyes went immediately to the foreground image, which they spent most of the time studying. In contrast, the Chinese usually went first to the background— a meadow or forest, for example—exploring it and only briefly glancing at the foreground image. Asked to recall what they had seen, the Americans more readily remembered the foreground objects, while the Chinese often forgot what was in the foreground but could recall the background in detail.

The contrast between these two thought patterns is significant for designers seeking to work with complexity. The "narrow gazing" of the Western perspective not only discounts the contextual relationships out of which change emerges, it reinforces the Cartesian bias that the world is a collection of measurable parts.

The Western tendency to be object or foreground oriented is not prima facie better or worse than the East Asian tendency to be context or background oriented. Each has strengths and weaknesses, depending on what one is working on. These habits become detrimental only when we are blind to them and, therefore, unable to direct our consciousness intentionally. "You might think you're thinking your own thoughts," Krishnamurti said some years ago, but "you're not. You're thinking your culture's thoughts."[8]

Pattern Literacy

Nisbett went on to develop his research further. He hypothesized that the Americans' focus on a central object meant that they were more likely to notice changes in objects but less likely to see changes in context, where it would be the opposite for the Chinese. He designed a second set of experiments, using short film clips to test where and how Westerners and East Asian students looked for and perceived change. Again, the conclusions were striking. Where Westerners were more likely to see changes in the focal, foreground objects, the East Asians noticed many more background differences and many more relationship differences.

Commenting on this research, Joshua Ramo said, "When it comes to the environment, Americans are almost completely change blind."[9] He advocated pursuing what, in Chinese philosophy, is often praised as the highest form of wisdom, *mastery of incipience*. As he described it, mastery of incipience is the ability to read context in order to know when change is going to begin. Regenerative development takes this thought further: It is also important to be able to see *where* change is coming from, and to understand *what* is sourcing it. The cognitive capability of "reading for change" is known as pattern literacy.

> It is also important to be able to see *where* change is coming from, and to understand *what* is sourcing it. The cognitive capability of "reading for change" is known as pattern literacy.

Pattern literacy was a core aspect of how indigenous people learned to understand the complexity of their world without simplifying it. Paula Underwood Spencer describes it this way:

> As a part of the Native American training I received from my father, one of the aspects of perception that I was asked to understand was the distinction between Hawk and Eagle, between the way Hawk perceives and the way Eagle perceives. In the shamanic tradition, you gain that appreciation by what is considered to be direct experience. However, the distinction—once learned—is easily translated into Western logical sequential language structure.

When hunting, Hawk sees Mouse . . . and dives directly for it.

When hunting, Eagle sees the whole pattern . . . sees movement in the general pattern . . . and dives for the movement, learning only later that it is a mouse.

What we are talking about here is Specificity and Wholeness.[10]

In his book, *Pattern Mind,* Joel Glanzberg points out the essential relationship between pattern literacy and the ancient art of animal tracking.

What is unseen is more powerful than what we see. Understanding requires seeing beneath the surface. This is not only true of abstractions like dignity and justice or the invisible genetic codes that determine so much of our lives, but also of these thoughts that you are reading right now, as if by magic through the visible letters on this page. Though, like a wild animal, my thoughts are long past, reading the tracks they left, you are watching them now, moving in your mind's eye.

Perceiving the deeper meanings behind all of the things we see in the physical world is the essence of tracking. It is about seeing not just the elements of the world, but the patterns of life. Tracking has taught me to see everything . . . as the lasting impressions left by the movements of life. . . . I have learned to look behind these lasting tracks that I can see so easily with my eyes to read the patterns of movement that left them.

Tracking patterns is always a matter of tracing trajectories—where things have come from (their source) and where they are headed (their goal). This is the only way to find where and how to intersect with living systems and to shift their trajectories.[11]

An ability to discern the patterns around us is key to honoring and working with complexity. "Western culture has spent decades drawing lines and boxes around interconnected phenomena," notes systems thinker Meg Wheatley, but "our safety and our future depend upon whether each of us can step outside our boxes and participate intelligently in a complex world of inter-connections."[12] It is this way of seeing that enables us to engage with a world that is becoming.

AIM THREE: BE A WORK IN PROGRESS

Thoughts and emotions are strongly influenced by cultural conditioning and the energy fields within which they arise. Unless we engage consciously with our own thinking processes, we run on tracks that have been laid down for us by our individual and collective pasts. The good news, as Mohandas Gandhi pointed out, is that "As human beings, our greatness lies not so much in being able to remake the world . . . as in being able to remake ourselves."[13]

Quantum physicist David Bohm often talked about how thought creates the world and then covers its tracks, allowing us to remain unconscious of our participation in shaping reality.[14] Unexamined systems of thought (our assumptions and values) shape our perceptions, reactions, and decisions, essentially creating a box within which our lives unfold. Psychologist R. D. Laing described the challenge this way: "The range of what we think and do is limited by what we fail to notice. And because we fail to notice what we fail to notice, there is little we can do to change; until we notice how failing to notice shapes our thoughts and deeds."[15]

Changing thinking is not like changing clothing—it is not a one-time event. It requires a practice of reflection. First, one must learn to see the process by which a thought is being shaped, even as the thought is forming. Observing one's own thinking *as it is happening* is a challenge that calls for discipline in the form of continuous engagement. Second, one must learn to manage being; and in order to manage being, one needs to conceptualize the existence of a self that is more than the sum of one's thoughts and feelings. We must become intentional with regard to the being we are producing in any given situation.

Self-Observing and Self-Remembering

One can improve the management of one's being through the interrelated practices of self-observing and self-remembering. Together, these practices help one avoid reactivity, which can so easily obscure what is actually important in a particular situation.

When self-observing, one maintains consciousness of three things: one's state, how it is being created, and the influence it is having on one's behavior and environment. The idea is to observe the extent to which unconscious habits or mechanical patterns are dictating behavior. Sustaining this consciousness, or regaining it when it has been lost, requires will and mental discipline.

When self-remembering, one holds in mind who one wants to be in a given situation, the self that is required to generate a higher order result. Humans are enormously flexible. We have far greater range for expression than we generally realize or are willing to admit. We can consciously choose to take on a role that is specific to our context and purpose, and play it in order to help realize the potential that we see. For this reason, members of Regenesis regularly prepare for a meeting or engagement by asking, "Who do I need to be in this situation?"

Self-observing and self-remembering require differentiating the self into three levels: the doer, the observer, and the self that sets an aim. By separating out an observing self ("I" in Figure 9.1), one can observe the patterns of doing and how those patterns relate to the effect being generated. The work of the observing self provides information that the aim-generating self—the "me" that one seeks to become—can draw on to actualize the value one is trying to create.

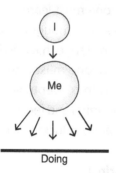

FIGURE 9.1 Self-observing and self-remembering requires differentiating the self into three levels.
Copyright © Regenesis Group, Inc.

Learning to sustain self-observing and self-remembering takes time and discipline. It is easy to get caught up in the drama of the moment and lose track of oneself. With practice, it becomes more and more a natural part of one's work. The key is to have patience and compassion, observing without judgment.

AN INVITATION

The role of human beings on Earth needs to shift. We must transform from despoilers to co-evolvers. This will require profound changes in the ways we inhabit our planet, our interactions with its material and spiritual resources. Equally, it will require profound changes in who we are as individuals. We must relearn how to think like natural systems and then act accordingly. In other words, our outer and inner work must advance together, each supporting the other.

In this book, regenerative development has been consistently presented as having an outer and inner dimension. The outer development of urban and rural places must always be matched by an inner development of those who will inhabit them. At the same time, the outwardly oriented work of planners and developers must be matched by inner reflection and commitment to true understanding.

In this book, regenerative development has been consistently presented as having an outer and inner dimension.

For those who wish to practice the art of regenerative development, the need is especially compelling. We have committed ourselves to a catalytic role, sparking the processes of transformation. This requires foresight, patience, tolerance for ambiguity, and sensitivity to unseen patterns. It asks that we become humble listeners and co-creators, and also fierce advocates for the unexpressed potential of every person, community, and living system that we encounter. Most of all, it requires us to manage ourselves—to maintain faith, steadiness, and a willingness to serve as instruments for a better future for every living being. We must learn to take sustenance from the processes of change because the products of what we seek to create may take generations to realize.

In the age of the Anthropocene, we are invited to regenerate ourselves as integrated, creative participants in the community of Earth.

In the age of the Anthropocene, we are invited to regenerate ourselves as integrated, creative participants in the community of Earth.[16] We must bring our whole selves to the task. Our sciences, intuitions, arts, disciplines, experiences, natures, and capacity for dreams—all will be needed if we are to answer the calling we've been given.

ENDNOTES

1. Kathia Laszlo, "From Systems Thinking to Systems Being," a blog post at Saybrook University, Rethinking Complexity, Studying Systems for a Humane and Sustainable World, July 24, 2011 (accessed August 31, 2015), www.saybrook.edu/rethinkingcomplexity/posts/07-24-11/systems-thinking-systems-being.
2. Abraham H. Maslow, "A Theory of Human Motivation," *Psychological Review* 50, 1943, p. 383.
3. Abraham H. Maslow, *Toward a Psychology of Being* (New York: Von Nostrand Reinhold, 1968).
4. Nicholas Mang, Toward a regenerative psychology of urban planning, Saybrook Graduate School and Research Center, San Francisco, 2009 http://gradworks.umi.com/33/68/3368975.html and http://powersofplace.com/papers.htm.
5. James Hillman and Michael Ventura, *We've Had a Hundred Years of Psychotherapy and the World's Getting Worse* (New York: HarperCollins Publishers, 1993).
6. Saint-Exupéry didn't actually say this: http://quoteinvestigator.com/2015/08/25/sea/.
7. Paula Underwood Spencer, "A Native American Worldview—Based on a Presentation to the Board of Directors of The Institute of Noetic Sciences," *Noetic Sciences Review,* Summer 1990.
8. Krishnamurti, quoted by Nora Bateson in *An Ecology of Mind* (Reading, PA: Bullfrog Films, 2011).
9. Joshua Ramos, *The Age of the Unthinkable: Why the New World Disorder Constantly Surprises Us and What We Can Do About It* (New York: Little, Brown and Company, 2009).
10. Paula Underwood Spencer, ibid.
11. Joel Glanzberg, *Pattern Mind* (Berkeley: North Atlantic Books, 2016).
12. Margaret Wheatley, "Webs, Boxes and Boundaries," posted at Mindful, August 26, 2010 (accessed August 31, 2015) www.mindful.org/webs-boxes-and-boundaries/.
13. Mohandas K. Gandhi.
14. David Bohm and Mark Edwards, *Changing Consciousness: Exploring the Hidden Source of the Social, Political, and Environmental Crises Facing Our World* (San Francisco: HarperCollins, 1992).
15. R.D. Laing, quoted in Margaret Ann Crain, Joseph V. Crockett, and Jack L. Seymour, *Educating Christians: The Intersection of Meaning, Learning, and Vocation* (Nashville, TN: Abingdon Press, 1993).
16. The Anthropocene is a term widely used to denote the present time interval in which many geologically significant conditions and processes are profoundly altered by human activities. For more information, visit http://quaternary.stratigraphy.org/workinggroups/anthropocene/ (accessed August 31, 2015) and http://goodanthropocenes.net (accessed August 31, 2015).

EPILOGUE

*Another world is not only possible, she's on her way, and on a quiet day,
if you listen very carefully, you can hear her breathing.*[1]

Arundhati Roy

We have set our common home on fire and to move forward we must first put out the flames. But this is only a first step. In and of itself it will not mark the arrival of a new world. It will not change the mindsets that have used Earth's abundance to strip away her biocultural diversity. It will not restore the basis of life's creativity. And it will not seed the new role for humans that a new world requires.

Happily, these changes are the topic of a quiet but ubiquitous conversation. It has been unfolding for some time, not in the media spotlight but in millions of neighborhoods, communities, and grassroots projects around the world. It is happening locally, wherever people are joining together to redesign how they work and live.

BLESSED UNREST

Paul Hawken captured the global scale of this conversation in his 2008 book *Blessed Unrest*. He called it the largest social movement in all of human history, involving "tens of millions of people dedicated to change."[2] It is a movement without a leader, arising from the bottom up, with each project or organization formed around the particulars of a place.

At the heart of regenerative development is the belief that we *must* work from place. From this perspective, the main theme of this book is not particularly complicated—know your place and know who you are. The power to create a new world comes from putting these two together. And this requires radically new thinking and language.

As the movement that Hawken described matures, it is moving away from its early isolationist tendencies, which were an understandable reaction to the perceived threat of global monocultures. It is reinventing localism, re-conceptualizing places as nodes within open networks of exchange. Wolfgang Sachs called this *cosmopolitan localism*, localism that "seeks to amplify the richness of a place while keeping in mind the rights of a multifaceted world. It cherishes a particular place, yet at the same time knows about the relativity of all places."[3]

Cosmopolitan localism understands that real wealth comes from exchanges between places whose inhabitants nurture and evolve their distinctive qualities. It recognizes that places are co-creations of humans and nature. To quote Sachs again:

> The pursuit of space-centered unity is turning into the search for place-centered diversity. After all, it is only from places that variety crops up, because it is in places that people weave the present into their particular thread of history. Thus, native languages are beginning to be revalued, traditional knowledge systems rediscovered, and local economics revitalized.[4]

The search for place-centered diversity provides an unprecedented opportunity to create a new story about what it means to live sustainably. Place offers a source of collective meaning, identity, and wellbeing. Within this context, the requirements of sustainable inhabitance can converge to create new practices and a new culture.

A NEW ROLE FOR DESIGN

In the past, design has been thought of primarily as a problem-solving process. But design also plays the role of making meaning. Historian Victor Margolin describes the work of design as "the social construction of meaning."[5]

Design strategist Ezio Manzini argues, "Design is concerned with making sense of things—how they ought to be in order to create new meaningful entities."[6] This assigns to designers the critical role of enabling a new culture of sustainability rooted in place. As futurist Erich Jantsch puts it, "The act of design is an evolution of norms."[7]

One of the implications of the new localism is that people from all walks of life are coming together to reinvent their work and their places. They are becoming citizen designers. For design professionals, this opens up opportunities to place their skills in service to a host of disciplines and community aspirations.

Even more critical to the evolution of a new culture is the shaping of what artists Helen and Newton Harrison call "conversational drift." This is co-design as social conversation, developing distributed intelligence out of a deepening understanding of place. Such discourse creates a field within which guilds and nodal interventions can emerge, leveraging the influence of designers far beyond their direct involvement.

The starting thesis of this book was that there are three active design agents that can be employed in evolving a new culture:

- Design products, which continue to shape their environments
- Design processes, which evolve the thinking and values of direct participants while generating larger fields of influence
- Designers, who develop the inner capabilities required for emergent and co-creative processes

Within the context of regenerative development, designers evolve beyond problem solvers. They become resources for reconnecting places and people to their inherent potential. As such, they facilitate learning and develop the capacity of local citizen designers. By collaborating in the creation of shared images and stories, they help make tangible what sustainable well-being is in specific places. When they are most successful, their radical insights can evolve the questions people are asking and the goals they are pursuing. In short, regenerative practitioners are conscious and highly skilled agents of systems transformation.

This book has provided the most basic premises and principles of regenerative development. In order to bring them alive, it is necessary to integrate them into the design and implementation of place-sourced projects. Those who take on this work become contributors to the development of methodologies based in the principles of living systems. Their reward is the development of the skills and intelligence needed to address the most urgent issues of our time.

ENDNOTES

1. Arundhati Roy, "Confronting Empire," a speech presented at the World Social Forum in Porto Allegre, Brazil, January 27, 2003 (accessed August 31, 2015), www.youtube.com/watch?v=uu3t8Z-kavA.
2. Paul Hawken, *Blessed Unrest: How the Largest Social Movement in History Is Restoring Grace, Justice, and Beauty to the World* (New York: Penguin Books, 2008).
3. Wolfgang Sachs, editor, *The Development Dictionary: A Guide to Knowledge as Power* (London: Zed Books, 2010).
4. *Ibid.*
5. Victor Margolin, *The Politics of the Artificial: Essays on Design and Design Studies* (Chicago: University of Chicago Press, 2002).
6. Ezio Manzini, *Design, When Everybody Designs: An Introduction to Design for Social Innovation* (Cambridge: MIT Press, 2015).
7. Erich Jantsch, *Design for Evolution: Self-Organization and Planning in the Life of Human Systems* (New York: George Braziller, Inc., 1975).

FURTHER READING

Understanding How Living Systems Work

Gregory Bateson

Steps to an Ecology of Mind, Ballantine, 1972; *Mind and Nature: A Necessary Unity*, Ballantine, 1979

Fritjof Capra

The Web of Life: A New Scientific Understanding of Living Systems, Anchor Books, New York, 1996

Elisabet Sahtouris

"Earthdance: Living Systems in Evolution," www.ratical.org/LifeWeb/ Erthdnce/

Seeing New Role and Potential of Humans

Thomas Berry

The Great Work—Our Way into the Future, Bell Tower, 1999

Wendell Berry

What Are People For? Counterpoint Press, 2010; *The Gift of Good Land,* North Point Press, 1981

René Dubos

A God Within: A Positive Approach to Man's Future as Part of the Natural World, Macmillan Publishing Co., 1972

Peter Forbes

"What Is a Whole Community and Why Should We Care?," www. wholecommunities.org/publications/

Daniel Imhoff

Farming with the Wild: Enhancing Biodiversity on Farms and Ranches, University of California Press, 2003

Aldo Leopold

A Sand County Almanac, Oxford University Press, 1949

Nicholas Mang

"The Rediscovery of Place and Our Human Role within It," Saybrook Graduate School and Research Center, 2006, http://powersofplace.com/papers.htm

David W. Orr

The Nature of Design: Ecology, Culture, and Human Intention, Oxford University Press, 2002; *Earth in Mind: On Education, Environment, and the Human Prospect,* Island Press, 2004

E. O. Wilson

Biophilia, Harvard University Press, 1984

Perspectives on Design
Janine Benyus

Biomimicry, William Morrow, 1997

Dominique Hes and Chrisna du Plessis

Designing for Hope: Pathways to Regenerative Sustainability, Routledge, 2015

Erich Jantsch

Design for Evolution: Self-Organization and Planning in the Life of Human Systems, George Braziller, 1975

Brad Lancaster

Rainwater Harvesting for Drylands and Beyond, Volumes 1 and 2, Rainsource Press, 2007 and 2013

John Tilman Lyle

Designing Human Ecosystems, John Wiley & Sons, 1984; *Regenerative Design for Sustainable Development*, John Wiley & Sons, 1994

Ezio Manzini

Design, When Everybody Designs: An Introduction to Design for Social Innovation, The MIT Press, 2015

Bill Mollison

Permaculture: A Designers' Manual, Tagari Publications, 1988

Sim Van der Ryn and Stuart Cowan

Ecological Design, Island Press, 1996

Understanding and Designing for Systems Change

M. Kat Anderson

Tending the Wild: Native American Knowledge and the Management of California's Natural Resources, University of California Press, 2005

David Bohm

With Mark Edwards, *Changing Consciousness: Exploring the Hidden Source of the Social, Political, and Environmental Crises Facing our World*, HarperCollins, 1991; with David Peat, *Science, Order and Creativity*, Routledge, 1987

John Hagel III, John Seely Brown, and Lang Davison

The Power of Pull: How Small Moves, Smartly Made, Can Set Big Things in Motion, Basic Books, 2012

Erich Laszlo

Introduction to Systems Philosophy: Toward a New Paradigm of Contemporary Thought, Harper Torch Books, 1973

Juan Ramo

Age of the Unthinkable: Why the New World Disorder Constantly Surprises Us and What We Can Do About It, Little, Brown and Company, 2009

Carol Sanford

The Responsible Business, Jossey-Bass, 2011

Nassim Nicholas Taleb

Antifragile: Things That Gain from Disorder, Random House, 2012

Andrew Zolli and Ann Marie Healy

Resilience: Why Things Bounce Back, Simon and Schuster, 2012

INDEX

Page numbers followed by *f* refer to figures.

223